The Safest Place Possible

A Guide to Healing and Transformation

Debbie Mirza

The Safest Place Possible. Copyright © 2016 by Debbie Mirza and Safe Place Publishing, Monument, CO

DebbieMirza.com

Author photograph by Abby Mortenson, Love Roots Photography

_____

Although the author and publisher have made every effort to ensure that the information in this book was correct at press time, the author and publisher do not assume and hereby disclaim any liability to any party for any loss, damage, or disruption caused by errors or omissions, whether such errors or omissions result from negligence, accident, or any other cause.

This book is not intended as a substitute for the medical advice of physicians. The reader should regularly consult a physician in matters relating to his/her health and particularly with respect to any symptoms that may require diagnosis or medical attention.

ISBN: 978-0-9986213-0-2
eISBN: 978-0-9986213-1-9

Acknowledgments

I have been blessed to have family and friends in my life that have provided such a safe place for me to be me.

To my Mom, who was the embodiment of love, compassion, and empathy. She was one of the greatest gifts I have experienced in this life. She was the definition of a safe place. I felt comforted by her presence, calmed by her soothing voice, and loved unconditionally. There are not enough words to express how grateful I am to have had the privilege of being her daughter.

To my Dad who took amazing care of her in her later years as she slowly declined due to dementia. I will love you forever for that Dad, and am immensely grateful for all the ways you have been there for me as well. I love that I still get to see you, to enjoy your hugs, and share our mutual love of travel and adventure. I love you and feel so blessed to have you as my Dad.

To my sister, Sonia Huenergardt. You have been a lifeline for me many times over. I love it when you launch into your profound, passionate, and full of wisdom speeches at just the right time. I cherish your big, tender heart and deep care for me. I am so grateful for so many things about you. Thank you for loving me so well. I feel incredibly lucky to have you in my life.

When I had kids, my top priority was to instill as solid a foundation as I could for them, like my Mom did for me. I knew I would be guiding them through life. I didn't expect to learn so much from them.

To my daughter Cassie, words cannot express how much I love you. You bring such a unique and refreshing view of life. I think I could write a book on that alone. You bring so much life wherever you go. You have opened my eyes to things I never would have seen had you not been in my life. I love being with you, traveling with you, listening to your thoughts and ideas, head-banging in the car with you, making our favorite Christmas cupcakes with you, and going on adventures with you by my side. I'm so grateful you are in my life lovely one.

To my son Curtis, you are such a delight. I love how you have a mind of your own. I love your passionate and enthusiastic heart. You are a change maker with a lot of power behind you. I love hearing your thoughts and look forward to seeing how you change things for the better in this world. You already have just by being you. I love having you in my life. I love your honesty, your uniqueness, your drive, your depth, and your comments that make me laugh so much. I think you and Cassie make me laugh more than anyone. I'm so grateful for you Curtis.

I didn't grow up with extended family in the same area for most of my life, but have had the privilege of being around a beautiful group of big-hearted cousins in recent years. I love you Pagards! To Terry Pagard, who has been a great friend to me as well as family. Thank you for all the talks, all the times you listened to me, poured me wine when I felt out of sorts, had me over for dinner, sang with me, and made me laugh. One of my favorite things in life is listening to you and Kris Pagard play guitar and sing at family gatherings.

To Liz Brekelbaum. Oh wow. Where do I start? I start with tears I guess, because that's what is happening right now as I write this. You have been a consistently safe place for me for so many years now. You are so special. No matter what I was going through in life I have always felt your love, acceptance, and enjoyment of me. Your friendship means the world to me, Lizzy. I feel so incredibly blessed to have a friend like you. The world is so blessed to have you here. Your presence alone is healing.

To Sonja Yamin. You hold a very special place in my heart. I have a spiritual connection with you like no other. You usher me into a space that is so sacred and precious to me. You feel like a lifeline for my soul here. I am so grateful for all our talks. I love how we dive right in with each conversation. I cherish you, Sonja.

To Michelle Kingsbury. We became instant friends in seventh grade. I'm thinking it was my sense of style as I entered the classroom in my green velour V-neck shirt and red corduroy pants that made you want to be friends with me. Thinking about you brings a smile to my face. So many cherished memories Michelley. Thank you for being there for me so many times. Thank you for your big caring heart. You mean so much to me.

To Laura Blackburn. You were my first friend! I can't believe we now live only fifteen minutes from each other after first meeting in Beirut, Lebanon when we were babies. You are such a special friend to me. Thank you for caring about me, laughing with me, and being my movie-watching buddy. I love you, Laura.

To Ingrid Seymour. You are so special to me. You have been a shining light in my life from the moment I met you. Thank you for your belief in me, for your constant encouragement and unwavering love and support. Your home, your presence is such a safe space to me and I am so grateful to have you in my life lovely Ingrid.

Thank you to Crys Wood for so lovingly and carefully proofreading this book and tweaking things so it would be ready for publication. It was a joy to work with you.

And thank you to Michelle Vandepas and Camille Truman for helping me with so many little details to get this book out into the world and being such a great team to work with.

To all the angels and unseen helpers, I feel you, I sense you, and I thank you for all your help and unwavering love. I am beyond grateful for you.

And to you, dear reader. I adore you. I am so grateful for you. And I am thrilled at the thought of meeting you someday.

Table of Contents

Preface

I have learned something about life that has changed everything for me. It has transformed me and, as a result, life feels different now. I feel an underlying peace inside me, a calm that was not there before. A newfound strength has developed inside me, and life seems to flow with an ease that is the opposite of what I experienced for most of my life.

I want to share my journey with you, how I came to this state of being, knowing the profound peace and joy it will bring you as well.

The body we live in is our home.

The conditions inside ourselves affect the things we experience in life. The state of our mental and emotional body, more than our circumstances, determines the degree to which we enjoy this life or find it to be utterly frustrating and disappointing.

We live here. We feel what it is like to be in this body every second. Most of us don't allow ourselves to feel what is going on inside because it can be an emotionally scary place to live. The thoughts in our head and what we do with those thoughts can lead us to feel unsafe and unhappy in this world.

Making my physical home a place that feels safe like a refuge—a dwelling where I can be myself, kick my feet up, and relax—has always been a priority to me throughout my life.

What I've realized is I have not done the same thing with my body as I have with my physical home. I have not created a place that feels safe for me to exist in.

I realized this on a much-needed trip to Bali. This awakening launched into a year of relearning how to be with myself, how to create the safest space possible to live in.

I was guided to several ways of doing this, to new thinking patterns, a new way of being with myself.

I transformed into someone I love living with. The peace I experience now, the stillness, the quiet within me—even when circumstances haven't lined up like I thought I would need them to for me to feel happy—has been an extraordinary experience.

What I have learned, the changes that have occurred in me, have been so life-changing that I want to share my experiences with you in the hope that they would bring you to a whole new relationship with yourself.

This book is a collection of stories from my own experiences, my journey of creating the safest space possible for me to live in. These pages also share thoughts about life that have shifted the way I think and behave, and have brought about a new relationship with myself and the world I live in.

This journey of mine took place about a year after I experienced a painful divorce. You will hear stories about me healing from that and learning to take care of myself while trying to figure out how to build a new life.

I also share wisdom I have learned through being a life coach, things I have seen work for myself and others.

This book can also be used for inspiration, love and wisdom when you are looking for guidance in a certain area of your life. You don't have to read it in order. If you are feeling down or struggling with something one day, you can ask to be led to the perfect chapter for you, randomly open the book, and then read whatever chapter opens up for you.

It is my belief that just reading this book will change you in some way, even if you don't do any of the exercises or use any of the tools I mention. The words will shift things inside you, bringing you more peace and ease-of-life no matter your circumstances.

If you are going through a difficult time in your life right now, I hope this will be a book that holds you, carries you through, helps bring about a lightness and feelings of freedom and hope inside you.

If you are feeling angst in your life, more anxiety than you would like, I promise you there is another path that feels very different. I hope the words on these pages lead you there, my love.

I feel a kinship with you already.

I hope we can meet someday and I can hear your story.

Read on, lovely, and feel yourself getting closer to the beautiful soul inside you that is ready to feel peace.

1

The Safest Place Possible

The night before I left for Bali, I had a vision.

I saw a girl running through a field chasing a butterfly. She looked happy, free, playful. It felt like some kind of foreshadowing, something to do with my upcoming trip, but I wasn't sure what it meant.

Over the past couple of years I've experienced the painful dissolution and ending of a marriage I thought I'd be in for the rest of my life, the death of my beloved mom, moving my kids and myself to a new city, many hours of therapy, massive amounts of tears and confusion, lawyers, mediation, and trying to figure out what to do with my life after years of being a stay-at-home mom.

I put lots of effort into rebuilding my life but got to a point of overwhelm where I felt like I'd hit a wall and couldn't function anymore. I had no desire to function anymore. I felt exhausted, passionless, and lost.

The only thing I felt like doing was running away. Far, far away. I felt like going somewhere that felt totally different than

America. A place where no one knew me, where I could stare at rice fields for as long as I needed to.

Deciding to actually pursue this idea, I asked for divine help and doors started opening. I was offered a place to stay for free in Ubud, Bali. Plane tickets were less than I had ever seen before. My Dad agreed to stay with my kids while I left for a couple of weeks on my own. I had not been on my own like that, I think, ever. I had never gone to a new country completely by myself, knowing no one. But something about it felt so perfect. So inviting. I felt like I would finally be able to take a breath, to sit and just be with myself.

I didn't make any plans for my time there, except if I was going all that way I did want to meet Ketut Liyer, the medicine man that Elizabeth Gilbert spent so much time with and wrote about in her book *Eat, Pray, Love*. Other than that, my plan was just to stare at rice fields and cry for as long as I needed.

After a few days settling into my new environment, it was time to meet the now-famous medicine man. I was surprised by how easy it was to get in to see him. I just wandered right in with no appointment and there he was, sitting on a platform in front of his home.

He was much older than I expected. His eyes were closed. He looked very serious, almost stern.

A man approached me and explained that both he and Ketut would be meeting with me, but he would be the one doing the session as Ketut's memory was not as sharp as it used to be. When I sat next to Ketut, his eyes opened, and his face lit up, forming the warmest, biggest smile that breathed life into my soul. He took hold of my hands and said with eyes wide open and enthusiasm in his voice, "You are so beautiful."

There was something about his hands that felt so warm to me, so authentic, so tender. I would have loved to hold onto them all day. I was disappointed that I wouldn't be getting a reading from him, but that feeling quickly left when the other man started talking. He knew nothing about me yet looked into my eyes and said, "In this life you will have two marriages. Last man, not good… Not good for your heart." His forehead tightened as if he was in pain and he said, "Very confusing, this man. Very difficult for you."

My eyes welled up with tears. With all the therapy I had been through and the long talks with wonderful life coaches over the past couple of years, there was something so healing about the simplicity of what he said and his tender delivery.

After reading my palms and telling me different things about my life, he lifted his hand in front of me and said with urgency in his voice, "You must take care of your heart. When your heart happy, more happy come to you." He went on to say other things but kept coming back with concern in his face saying, "You must take care of your heart." This seemed to be his main message to me, delivered with great love and concern. It felt like he couldn't repeat this enough. I felt a strong sense that if I remembered nothing else from our time, I must remember this.

His words kept repeating in my mind for the rest of the day: *You must take care of your heart.*

That night, I found myself lying down in the corner of my room on the wood floor, curled up in the fetal position, releasing deep tears that were begging to be heard. I realized I was grieving more than the loss of the marriage. These tears felt like they went back much further.

I was grieving so many years of not taking care of my heart. I reflected on all the times my kind and tender heart tried to guide me, only to be ignored or silenced. All the times I talked myself out of listening to it. So many years of not trusting it, of thinking other people knew what I needed more than I did. Believing someone else was more of an expert than me. Being influenced by those with louder voices and stronger opinions.

This left me unsure of myself. It left me feeling ungrounded and unsafe, feeling utterly lost and scared about life on my own.

In that moment I started to see my heart as a young girl who had not been allowed to freely be herself. It seemed like she had been caged, contained for a long time.

I spoke to her that night and said, "I am so sorry. I am so very sorry for all the times I didn't let you feel whatever you were feeling and say whatever you wanted to say. For all the times I put other's opinions before yours. I'm sorry for all the ways I tried to talk you out of what you were feeling. I want to make a vow to you right now that things are going to be different. I will listen to you more. I will respect what you say and how you feel. I promise you I am going to work on this relationship. I owe you this."

The next morning I was sitting out on the deck in front of my room overlooking the rice fields nearby, and a large butterfly came to visit, just like it had the previous few mornings.

It flew around the same tree, right in front of me, at about the same time each morning. I had never seen such a large butterfly. I grabbed my phone to try to film it. Slowly creeping up, I was able to capture this beautiful creature. Feeling so excited, I watched the footage and started to cry when I heard myself on the video whispering playfully, "I'm trying to catch the butterfly." The vision came back to me. I was the girl chasing a butterfly, the girl in me that wanted to be free.

When I got home, a new way of being with myself became my top priority. Over time I changed the way I am with myself. I embarked on a journey that led to beautiful changes in me and in my world I did not expect.

I knew I needed to create the safest space possible to live in, a place where my heart was heard and well taken care of.

After Bali, I found I lost all interest in books and other people's opinions and knowledge. It all felt like clutter in my mind. I needed time to hear just me. It became a sacred time of going within.

I lost interest in outside stimulus. I stayed home a lot. I went into nature a lot.

I was guided to do different things, to think in different ways, and it changed my life dramatically.

I've always been one to gravitate to self-help books, always been a seeker of healing and truth. I've tried many things throughout my life, but I have never seen myself change in such a deep and profound way before.

I noticed at one point that the mean girl inside my head was gone. *Gone.* You know the voice inside most of us that can be so cruel, putting down the way we look, telling us what we do and don't deserve? Criticizing? Gone. I have not heard a negative message about myself from my head for almost a year now.

The things I have discovered and practices I have adopted have been changing the very foundation of me. I find myself being more present than ever without trying to be. It has become a natural way of being for me.

I feel more love for myself, others, animals, bugs, rocks, trees, and everything around me than ever before. When I feel joy and happiness now, it feels bigger than it used to. It has a depth and rootedness to it. I notice I laugh more than I have in years.

The direction I want to go in my life has become crystal clear after years of feeling lost and wondering what to do with it.

A newfound trust has developed in me. Things seem to work out magically for me more than ever before. Synchronicities have increased.

The energy of life feels like it has shifted from pushing hard and going after things to flowing with things and seeing them come to me. I'm living from inspired, fulfilling action rather than action from a place of fear.

My need for people to like and approve of me has substantially lessened.

I wrote this book to share my journey with you in the hope that it will help you create the safest place possible for you to live in. If you choose to change the environment in your body, to create an emotionally safe space for your heart, your life will change—I promise you that. You will experience more peace and more calm than you can imagine. You will connect with yourself in a whole new way.

When we create a safe space, our nervous system is able to relax. Our energy changes, which in turn changes the energy around us. Healing takes place inside us and affects those around us as well, in the best way possible.

This book is a collection of things I did to help myself create a refuge to live in. It is also a memoir of my journey of transformation and awakening.

I wrote this book for you because I love you, and I want you to feel more love than you thought humanly possible. It is also a love letter for your heart, your precious, well-deserving heart.

You must take care of your heart. When your heart happy, more happy come to you.

I hope that reading this book brings you peace, calm, and a new relationship with yourself and the world around you.

Much love to you on your own beautiful journey.

The Safest Place Possible

2

Effortless Value

Bali was filled with gorgeous flowers and lush greenery everywhere. I remember staring at one particular flower, at one point, noticing every detail of it. I looked at its beautiful colors, the artistic lines in its leaves, its shape that was so perfectly formed. I was mesmerized by this beautiful work of art.

It struck me how effortless its existence was. It didn't work hard to grow. It didn't formulate a five-year plan to be where it was today. There was no goal setting, creating a life full of impressive accomplishments. It didn't need to do anything to try to be valuable. Its existence alone brought me peace, joy, and a sense of calm and wonder. Just by being there in its presence, I felt changed.

It didn't do anything to be that beautiful either. There was no working out three times a week to get and keep its stunning shape. Disciplining itself to stay off gluten was not needed, and it would never dream of having anything altered to make itself look better. Any change to its appearance would feel cruel and be totally unnecessary. It wouldn't make any sense to do that. It would feel almost violent.

It also didn't need me to look at it for it to know it was wanted.

The flower didn't need to do anything to bring beauty to this world. Just the fact it was here and I got to be around it brought tears to my eyes that morning. It calmed me, gave me a picture and a feeling of how effortless nature is and how little we need to do here to have a profound effect.

It wasn't worried about why it was here: Was it good enough? Was it too much?

It was perfect. It was providing so much to this world just by existing.

We tend to believe we need to be doing something on this planet to be of any value. The interesting thing is when I think of my favorite people in the world I realize that just knowing they are in this world helps me feel more relaxed.

I recently spent some time with my friend, Sonja, in Portland. There were many times we would sit beside each other in silence. Just being in her presence calms me, centers me. I feel my consciousness expanding when I am around her. Shifts in my thinking occur. I feel reassured. I feel valuable and totally accepted. I can feel she is happy I am here without her saying a word. She doesn't have to do anything for me to feel this way. Just who she is has an effect on me. If she does absolutely nothing in this life, chooses just to be here, she would be helping the earth and anyone that gets to be around her. Not everyone in her life recognizes this, but that doesn't mean it's not true.

Not everyone will recognize your beauty, your value, but that is not a barometer for truth. Trust me when I say you bring something unique and wanted to this world just by being in it. If you do nothing else while you're here, you've done enough.

When I was in my early twenties, I had candida. Because of it, I experienced depression and chronic fatigue. During the early stages, I would get up, brush my teeth, and have to go back to bed. It drained the life out of me, and it took a year to get it fully out of my system and to feel normal again. During the worst of it, my faithful friend, Michelle, called me. I cried on the phone telling her how useless I felt. I felt like I was taking up space. I had plans for my life. I wanted to help people. I was of no use to anyone anymore. She said, "Debbie, if you do nothing else in your life, just by being here it's enough."

My mom was never about my accomplishments either. She wasn't a mom that pushed me to get good grades or drove me to achieve success. She would say things like, "I hope you always stay this tender." That is what she valued more than what I did in this life. Being in the same room with her soothed me. Holding her hand felt like a special gift.

Oh, I hope you know how lovely you are, dear reader. I hope you know that just your being here is enough.

3

Beauty of Emotions

Emotions scare us almost more than anything else, when you think about it. We may think we are scared of running out of money and being homeless, but really it's the fear and anxiety we think we will feel if that happens that scares us.

We think we're scared of never having the size body we want, but really we are scared of always feeling bad about the way we look.

We think we're scared of not succeeding, but really we're scared of how we will feel if we don't.

We live our lives trying to avoid the emotions that feel bad and to experience the "good ones" as much as possible.

But what if we could make peace with all our emotions and were able to see them all as "good"? What if there were no bad or scary emotions? What if we could embrace each one as a friend? How would that change the way we feel, the way we experience life?

I have come to see that every emotion has a purpose and brings its own special gift to us. I'd like to talk through some of these and give you a picture of a recent experience that shifted the way I think about this part of being human.

Let's take a look at anger. Depending on how you were raised, there can be a lot of shame associated with this emotion. But anger can bring good things. Anger can spur you on to make a change. It can push you to stand up for something you believe in. It can move you to stop a cycle of abuse. Anger can help you feel alive. It can move you to take action, to help others.

What if we choose to embrace it, to feel every bit of it, to allow it to bring out of us what is ready to come out? What if we see anger as our friend, trying to help us move in a direction that will free us and benefit others?

How about grief? My mom left this earth two years ago. I'm not sure when, or if, I will ever be done grieving that loss. I don't know that anyone could fill her shoes or if I would want them to. You know what I love about grief? It connects me to her. It lets me feel that connection even though I can't put my arms around her. It allows me to feel her tenderness, to see her smile in my mind, to have a moment where I remember her love. When I feel grief, I feel tenderness, which brings my heart to a peaceful place.

Sadness. Here's one we really try to avoid but, when I think about it, sadness plays an essential role in my life, and I'm so grateful for it. When I am sad, and I allow myself to feel it, I am very present, very in my body. There is something that feels really good about staying with the sadness. Staying in my body, not trying to run from the feeling, not trying to change my mood. When I remain here with this feeling, it feels nurturing, cleansing, in a way. Allowing myself to be with it feels like I am taking care of myself, taking care of some part of me that needs me to be with it.

These are the minor chords in music that actually help us get in touch with parts of ourselves that are wanting to be still. When I am deeply sad, when it feels like depression, it takes me to a place of not caring about things I normally stress over. It helps strip me of things that don't really matter in the grand scheme of life. It brings me to myself. It keeps me here and allows me to release tears that help me heal. Depression has played a large role in bringing me home to myself. When I feel depressed and stay with it, I feel connected to myself.

When I had times of depression, it ultimately made me more tender, present, compassionate to myself and others. I believe it can be a time in our lives that leads us to an awakened state. When we stay with it, we let ourselves know we are here, and that goes a long way in proving we can be trusted. When the little girl or boy within us sees that we aren't going anywhere, that this depression doesn't scare us anymore, trust is built, and peace and rest come when that trust is proven.

How about fear or anxiety? This is a big one. Personally, it's my least favorite. Sorry, Fear, nothing personal. Now, how can we make peace with fear?

When I feel fear, it feels like everything spins out of control inside me. My thoughts run crazy, imagining all kinds of future possibilities that magnify and increase the fear in me. As I am writing this, I can't help but start laughing. When I am in touch with myself—that higher, wiser part of myself—I am fully aware there is no reason for us to fear.

It makes me laugh because fear unravels me so much. I have a pretty calm demeanor. I was raised in a fairly controlled environment. There was no yelling in our home. Conversations were calm and well thought out. My personality is not high-strung. I value peace. I love to meditate. I like to have calm conversations where there is awareness of other's feelings.

I am very poised. I get nervous when I sing or speak in front of people, but no one can ever tell. I am able to keep my composure. In a crisis, I tend to stay calm.

But with fear, I lose my marbles. The rational, wise part of me leaves the building. When I think about it, it's one of the best things for me. When I allow myself to let it all out, whether that's spilling all my fears to a trusted friend or speaking out loud in my living room or in my car and letting my tears flow, I feel relieved. Being really honest about my fears helps release something in me. Letting myself voice all the crazy that is inside feels really good and is actually quite healing.

Fear squeezes something out of me, out of all of us. It also helps highlight beliefs we hold that are ready to be released, to be healed. When I feel fearful, I will try to get to what the fear really is. Sometimes naming it relieves pressure, other times I need to work the thought. I ask myself if it's really true. If you haven't heard of Byron Katie's thought-dissolving questions, they are worth looking up. I use her method a lot, and it has brought me a lot of relief.

How about jealousy? It is a beautiful gift for our soul. Jealousy most commonly strikes in my world while scrolling through Facebook and Instagram, and can really send me down a dizzying spiral of emotions: *How do they afford all those vacations? His life looks more interesting and exciting than mine. Her life looks like so much more fun than mine!*

The reason jealousy is a gift is because it helps us see what we really want. For instance, I never feel jealous of math teachers, engineers, doctors, attorneys, or truck drivers. But I do feel envious of people who travel a lot, people who have figured out how to make money and live anywhere, people who have figured out how to make money doing what they love, and raw foodists who have so much energy and amazing skin. These are clear clues of what I want in my life. They point to what I crave, and after I clear out all the discouraging thoughts that pop up to prevent me from going after my cravings, I am able to come up with plans and ideas of how I can create what I want. Jealousy helps bring clarity and direction to our lives. It's one of the best built-in life coaches we have.

Recently I've spent a lot of time just being with myself, allowing emotions to come to the surface. I have been changing what I do with those different feelings. I no longer see them as an enemy I am trying to get rid of. They are a part of me.

On slow walks behind my house, the more I gave myself permission to feel all my emotions, the more I started to feel almost bad that I had been so mean to them, trying to rush them out the door and quickly replace them with good emotions. So I gave them permission to stay as long as they needed to.

I decided to welcome them in like they were old friends, like we'd had a rift for a long time, a family misunderstanding for years, and now after we had lived our lives and our kids were grown and gone we were in our retirement years and had almost forgotten what the fight had been about. We just didn't care anymore. It didn't matter.

The more I did this, the more I started to feel almost nurturing to my "guests". It was as if I was saying to each emotion, "Sorry I've been so hard on you. You can stay as long as you need. I don't really feel like figuring out why you're here. I just want you to know that it's okay that you are. Would you like some tea?"

It felt like the battle was over. I wasn't trying to get anywhere. I was just here in my body experiencing whatever came up. The more I did this, the more I noticed waves of happiness coming through me that had a depth to them, a groundedness. It wasn't fleeting. It was a part of me now.

When you meet each emotion with love and acceptance, when you let their energy run through you instead of trying to block them, there is a paradigm shift that occurs within you that will start affecting everything inside and outside of you in such a beautiful way. You will fear less in life because you will know that no matter what happens to you, the inside of you is safe and a loving place to be.

The chatter in your mind will lessen. You will feel more peace. You will be more present and able to love those around you with a healthy, selfless love, the purest form of love.

I hope this chapter brings relief to you in knowing there is no emotion that needs to be feared. Each one is here to help you in some way. When we embrace and accept every emotion that arises in us we connect with ourselves in a very powerful way. Living this way changes us, makes us more present, more tender, and more at peace.

May you embrace all your feelings today. May you be with yourself in a whole new way, knowing you are beautiful just the way you are. You are colorful and salty, and I'm so glad you're here.

4

My Teenage Sensei

It had been two years since my ex-husband and I sat on the beach behind the Shoreline Inn in Cayucos, California, and I heard him say the heart-shattering words, "I don't know if I want to be married to you anymore."

Thirteen months later our twenty-two-year marriage came to an end. This was something I never imagined happening in my life. It was an agonizing, confusing, and painful year, to say the least.

I knew someday I would come back to that beach as part of my healing process, as well as for my kids'. The time had come.

The three of us drove from Colorado to California and found the spot on the beach where our lives had taken a dramatic turn.

Over the past couple of years, I had been trying to figure out what to do with my wedding ring. After going to different jewelry stores to see what it was worth, and finding out the most I could get for it was fifty dollars, selling it just felt meaningless. I loved that ring. It represented so much for me. I remember designing it together with the help of a jeweler. It was the beginning of something we were both excited about. A symbol of our love, our commitment. I remember the proposal and the romantic gesture of the ring. It didn't feel right to hand it over to a random stranger in a store for fifty bucks.

I took it to Bali thinking some inspired idea might come to me for a healing or releasing ceremony I could do there, but nothing came.

It had sat in my backpack ever since, waiting for inspiration to strike.

On the road trip there my kids expressed different ideas of what I could do with it.

When we arrived at the Shoreline Inn, I found the spot on the sand where the devastating conversation took place two years prior. Looking out at the ocean, I knew what I wanted to do.

Turning to my seventeen-year-old daughter, Cassie, standing next to me, I said, "I want to throw it in the ocean, and I want to do some kind of ceremony."

"Okay," she said. "Let's do this."

As we sat down on a perfectly formed mound of sand, as naturally as breathing she began to lead me through an experience I will never forget and will cherish forever.

"Mom," she said, "before you throw that ring, tell me everything you are releasing."

I started listing a few things. Cassie stopped me and said, "No, Mom. What are you REALLY releasing? Dig deeper."

"I guess that did sound kind of Hallmark-ish," I said.

I closed my eyes, tightly held on to the ring in my hand, and dug deep.

What was it I really wanted to let go of? Not only from the marriage but from everything. This was my chance to put it all out there.

"I'm letting go of having it be okay for me to be mistreated." Tears started to come.

"I'm letting go of believing I have to be perfect to be wanted.

"I'm letting go of doubting myself and my abilities.

"I'm letting go of hiding my strength and my smart mind.

"I'm letting go of having to censor what I really feel.

"I'm letting go of not trusting my own intuition.

"I'm letting go of believing what others think of me.

"I'm letting go of having to always be nice, positive, and kind.

"I'm letting go of my fears of shining.

"I'm letting go of relationships that are the illusion of love.

"I'm letting go of all shame.

"I'm letting go of any thought that says any part of me is unlovable.

"I'm letting go of believing what others say more than trusting my own feelings.

"I'm letting go of the belief that says my body needs to be a certain size to be wanted.

"I'm letting go of believing I have to do something to be valuable.

"I'm letting go of the belief that says I need to be any more or less than I am to be loved.

"Okay, Cass," I said, "I think I'm ready to throw it."

"Okay. Now, when you throw it be grateful for your past and for your present, the good and the bad. Now you can create the life you've always wanted. It's a blank slate, Mom. Your new beginning starts now. You can be whoever you want," she said with the wisdom of a sage.

Her words filled my heart.

I stood up, walked toward the ocean, stopped, looked at the ring, and said *"Thank you"*, feeling the words settle within my body. Walking into the water as far as I could, I quietly said, "I'm grateful for my past. I'm grateful for my present. And I'm grateful for my future."

Standing there a moment, I took a deep breath, stretched back my arm, and then threw the ring as far as I could.

I turned around to see my daughter sitting on our spot. Then I turned back to look at the ocean and heard a gentle voice say, *"Debbie. Keep walking. Don't look back."*

Walking toward the shore, I couldn't believe how light I felt. I didn't know how I would feel. It felt like I had let go of a heavy weight I had been carrying for a very long time.

I couldn't stop smiling.

Life felt different, somehow. I felt free.

5

Benefits of Hiding

Hiding is a way of holding ourselves
until we are ready to come into the light.

-From "Consolations" by David Whyte

There is a time for hiding.

Many societies, especially in the West, value productivity quite highly. Because of this, it is easy for some to see hiding as a negative thing, like avoidance or not facing things. The truth is when we feel the need to be quiet, to retreat, our body is speaking and letting us know what it needs. Usually when this happens, our soul is getting ready to move into new territory and needs this time to work on things that will be needed for what is coming.

As I write this, I am sitting in a tree house that hangs over the Columbia River in Washougal, Washington. Over the past few months, I have been feeling the urge to be by myself a lot. I haven't felt like being around people. The thought of taking in any stimulus from outside myself has felt like noise lately. I have felt the urge to be in nature a lot, quiet and still.

Most of my life I've been one who goes after things I get excited about. I have been trying to figure out what to do with my life, how to make money, hoping to find something that excites me so I can go after it. But, so far, I just feel like doing nothing.

While I've been doing a whole lot of "nothing", fearful thoughts have been coming up in me: *"You can't just do nothing! You're going to end up homeless, not able to support yourself! Fine! If you do nothing, just don't let it last too long. You need to do things that are productive. You need to build a career. You need to be smart with your time! If you do nothing, you'll end up aimlessly wandering for the rest of your life, not accomplishing anything, and then you'll get yourself in trouble. You can't trust yourself! You can't live life just going by what you feel like doing. Life doesn't work that way!"*

Even though I have this part of me that is scared and lashes out in long passionate fear-based speeches, I also have a higher voice within me that is filled with wisdom, love, and calm. This part of me knows how much I need this time to heal, to rebuild.

My heart, my soul, and my body are begging me to spend more time just being. I still have healing to do inside of myself. I feel like I need to get off the speeding train of busy-ness and noise. As I do more of this, I see and feel things changing inside. I feel shifts happening in my brain and heart with the way I think about myself, about life, about how the world works.

It may look and feel like I'm doing nothing but, in fact, I'm doing some of the greatest work on earth right now because as I heal myself, as I learn to love myself, begin a new relationship with me, my frequency is changing, my vibration is rising. My nervous system is calming down, and that affects not only me but all those around me. By healing myself, I am healing others and the earth. That's what happens when we take care of ourselves. Everything is energy, and when one person in a room is calm and centered, it affects everyone else in that room as well.

I look lost to many around me, but the truth is I finally have a chance to find myself when I drop the doing and sit with the being. When it is time for me to emerge back into society, I will be clearer about why I am here, what I am here to do. I will be coming from a place of groundedness, of connection. I will be solid in myself and will not be as affected by social programming, by common thinking that leads us astray, away from our true nature.

As I've allowed myself to spend more and more time hiding, doing a lot of just being, letting myself feel whatever comes up, learning to treat myself with the utmost kindness, I realize how crucial it is for me to hide for as long as I feel I need to. It feels like a necessary incubation period, a time to cocoon.

I am also seeing I really can trust myself. My body knows exactly what it needs. The more I sit with myself, the more comfortable I am becoming with every part of me. When that happens my body is finally able to relax. The more relaxed I am, the more at peace I become.

It has felt like a risky thing for me to take time off from life, but the more I do, the more I see how imperative it is.

There are so many inputs in our society it can become difficult to hear ourselves, our own guidance. We can get stuck in our heads, get caught up in the dramas of life, and miss the world of peace and fulfillment that exists inside us.

The more we take the time to go inside, to develop the safest place for us to live, the more we will experience all the things we long for: Peace. Connection. The absence of fear. Confidence. Relaxation. Joy.

Hiding has been the best decision for me in my life right now, being with myself in a way I don't think I have ever been before. It feels like I am building a solid foundation within me so when I am ready to come out I will walk this earth differently. I will feel more connected to it and naturally make life decisions that are inspired and directed from my heart and soul, my true self. I will know that no matter what happens in life, I will be okay because I now know I live in a body that will take care of me, that will meet me with love, tenderness, kindness, and emotional safety.

Hiding has helped me know to the depth of my being that I will never be alone.

If you are feeling overwhelmed by people, activities, or to-do lists, if you are feeling the need for quiet and a time of hiding, I hope you honor that. You will never regret taking that time.

I hope you will give yourself permission to hide if that's what you are craving right now.

I smile at thinking of you having that precious time with yourself. Let whatever needs to come up in you rise to the surface and meet it with love and kindness. Be with yourself as a great caretaker would. You deserve that.

May you have the courage to live your life in a way that feels relieving to your body. May you be able to see how much you can trust yourself. May you know that listening to your body, your heart, and your longings will lead you to a life you long to live.

Much love and kindness to you, special one.

6

Snow White and Rose Red

A few months after my divorce was final I went to a writers' retreat led by Betsy Rapoport, a life coach and accomplished writer and editor, as well as a super delightful person who makes me laugh whenever I'm around her.

One evening she invited her good friend Michael Trotta—a nature-based coach and a brilliant storyteller—to join us around a firepit in her backyard. He talked to us about the lost art of storytelling and how much we miss by not looking at the themes in fairy tales and other stories that help us see things about ourselves and life.

Around a perfectly formed fire, he told us the original version of Snow White and Rose Red. He asked us to notice any parts of the story that brought out an emotional charge in us. When he finished, I shared that I felt frustrated whenever the bear was in the scene. I didn't know if he could be trusted. He was kind, but I kept wondering if he was going to turn on the girls.

Throughout my life I have easily trusted people. Because of this, I have experienced deep and meaningful relationships, but with the people who weren't truly trustworthy, I have been hurt. Now I feel more wary of trusting after experiencing things as I did in my marriage.

Michael gave the story a twist when he told us all the characters are us. I realized then the message for me was realizing I was afraid to trust the prince in me (the bear turns out to be a prince), that male part of me. We all have male and female traits within us.

We each shared our thoughts with the group. After hearing me share my thoughts, Michael gently asked, *"Debbie, would you like to put more logs on the fire?"*

"Sure. I love building fires," I responded. I was a camp counselor for a couple of summers during college and got really good at building fires. I was kind of excited to show off my impressive fire building abilities.

I walked up and started to add four logs to the fire. I wanted to place them in a perfect teepee formation as Michael had, and how I had learned to at camp. Every time I tried, one of the logs would fall down, and the others would follow. I felt frustrated and self-conscious with everyone watching my failed attempts. Finally, I just carelessly threw the last log in, thinking, *Screw it.* I tried to tell myself it didn't matter, it didn't have to be perfect. But I felt embarrassed. I didn't know how to fix it. I sat down in the circle.

The group was quiet. Then Michael said, *"Debbie, how do you feel about the fire?"*

Part of me didn't want to talk about it. I was wishing we could just move on. I responded, *"I don't like it. It looks like a mess. It looks terrible."* In a normal situation, it wouldn't have mattered what my fire arrangement looked like, but I knew something was being triggered within me, clearly something deeper than my ability to place logs. I knew this picture represented something in my life that made me want to cry.

"I have a hunch you were never taught what to do with your fire," he said.

Those words hit me deeply. I knew what Michael meant, and he was right. I had been raised to be nice, to be nurturing, to be kind. I knew how to be Snow White. I was a natural at that, and I'm grateful for that. I wasn't taught how to deal with that fiery part of me. That part that feels so deeply and passionately. That fierceness I feel inside: the anger, the frustration, the boldness. I wasn't as comfortable being Rose Red. Snow White was easy for me.

Most people love Snow White and her sweetness. But not everyone responds positively to Rose Red, the fiery one who ran around shooting bows and arrows. I related to her, though, just like I felt a connection to the character of Katniss Everdeen in the book *The Hunger Games*, like so many women did. I actually love that side of me. It feels good, it feels alive, and the combination of the two is amazing.

"Debbie, do you want to redo the fire?" Michael asked, with a tone of full trust in my abilities.

"I would love to," I said. Rose Red in me stood up with a fierceness and determination I've felt before. I reached my hand into that hot fire, grabbed each log and attempted to create that perfect teepee formation. After the placement of each log, I shielded my eyes from the painful smoke pouring into them. It worked for three of the logs. The fourth was lodged in a way that, if I touched it, I would burn myself. I stood there contemplating what to do next. Jessica, who was sitting behind me, gently whispered, *"Snow White."* A tear came to my eye as I smiled. I knew what she meant. I needed that loving reminder. This was the time for the nurturing part of me to show up and protect me from hurting myself, from trying to make something the way I thought it should be.

At that point, Michael said I could use the smaller sticks below me if I wanted to. The logs had run out. I decided to forgo my plan to build what I thought would be a perfect fire and create a different configuration. I still set up the three logs in a triangle but in place of the fourth log, I placed a bundle of sticks.

The parallels to my marriage were staring me in the face as I stood there looking at the design I created. I tried to keep a family together but couldn't do it, and I'd reached a place where I had to come to grips with the fact it was over. The family unit that was once four no longer existed. It was now three, and I needed to figure out a way to make this new reality work. I resisted it for a long time and had a difficult time accepting this new life. I needed support from several others to make this new family paradigm work. I will be forever grateful for the people who stepped up to become the cluster of small pieces of wood for me and my two kids.

"What do you think of your fire now?" Michael asked.

I felt calm as I looked at it. *"I like it. It's creative. It looks interesting, unique."*

"And you know what I'm noticing?" he said. *"The heat is evenly distributed, it's not too big or too small. I am warmed by it but not too warm."*

Something about hearing that felt good to me.

"Look what happened when you let go of trying to make it perfect."

The fire in my life looks different now, and this new formation, as it turns out, is capable of burning brighter than I could have ever imagined.

Where in your life does Snow White need to show up for you? What about Rose Red?

What would your life look like if you were to let go of the "perfect" picture and build it in a way that works for you, that is suited for your beautiful self?

7

Ho'oponopono

I'm sorry. Forgive me. I love you. Thank you.

I say these words often. Many times I speak them over and over, and I can feel things shifting inside me when I do. They are powerful. They are words we've all heard before but in sequence, with intention, they clear out things inside us and bring us healing and freedom.

Years ago I read about a man, Dr. Ihaleakala Hew Len, a psychologist who single-handedly healed an entire ward of criminally insane patients without ever meeting them.

Dr. Len believed that we are all mirrors of each other and if he "cleaned" on himself things he unconsciously shared with someone else, the other person would experience healing as well. So he would look at an inmates' chart, then say, *"Forgive me, I'm sorry, I love you, Thank you"*. By saying this he believed he was clearing things out in himself and in turn clearing it out of the inmate.

I know. This is out there. Really out there thinking, but the amazing thing is after a few years of him doing this, never meeting the inmates face to face, all of the men changed. In fact, even the staff changed.

Before he came to the ward at Hawaii State Hospital psychologists were quitting on a monthly basis. It was a dangerous place filled with criminally insane inmates. The staff lived in fear of being attacked by the patients.

After a few months of Dr. Len being there, patients who had been shackled were now allowed to walk freely. Others who were on medication no longer needed it. Some were even set free. The staff began to actually enjoy coming to work. If you would like to learn more about Dr. Len I recommend the book *Zero Limits* by Joe Vitale.

The ancient Hawaiian healing method he used is called Ho'oponopono.

When you heal yourself, you heal others.

Taking full responsibility for everything inside you and loving each of these parts not only heals you, it also heals those around you.

By saying the phrase *"I'm sorry, please forgive me, I love you, thank you"* you are owning that there are things in you that need to be cleared out, and clearing them out through love. This applies to basically anything inside you that does not feel good to you. Any part of you that feels like it needs healing and freedom.

If I am angry with someone, hurt by someone, they are a mirror of what is going on inside me, and if I clear out whatever that is, I also help heal them. If I am triggered by something someone says to me that means there is some part of me that is agreeing with them.

For instance, if my neighbor said *"I think it's weird that your trash can is blue",* that wouldn't affect me because I am fine with the color of my trash can. But if someone was to tell me how difficult it is to lose weight after you turn forty, my stomach would tighten and fear would set in, because there is still a part of me that buys into that fear/belief that says my body is too big and it's going to be really hard for me to get to the size I want to be. This causes me emotional pain and gives me an opportunity to clear out these painful thoughts/feelings/vibrations/programs within me.

When I say, *"I'm sorry",* for me, I am saying I'm sorry for any pain I cause my body by believing these things and any other beliefs I'm not aware of that are causing me to feel emotional pain.

"Forgive me, I love you."—I really feel this when I say it, really letting these powerful words settle into my body—*"Thank you."*—

I'm saying this to the Universe, God, the Divine, my higher self for bringing this to my attention so I can have the opportunity to clear all this out of my body and heal.

The beautiful thing is you don't have to know what you are clearing. To do ho'oponopono, you don't have to know what the problem is. All you have to do is notice you are feeling something that doesn't feel good.

Dr. Len saw his own pain inside him as a shared memory with each patient. He saw it as a program that caused the person to act out the way they were. As he felt the program in himself, he cleaned. He saw it as neutralizing the energy he associated with that person. Then by saying the words he was allowing Divinity to come in and fill the void with pure light.

In my own experience, I have witnessed people's behavior change when I have done this. When my kids were younger there was a teacher I found difficult to work with, communicate with. I did ho'oponopono when I thought of her and, over time, I noticed she became kinder and very easy to work with.

I have also seen circumstances change after doing ho'oponopono.

When I was married and my husband and I were first learning about this, he experienced something that was miraculous and so unexpected. He worked for a large airline company and bid each month for the schedule he wanted for the following month. In November he forgot to bid for December's schedule, which meant he would be out of town for most of the month and would miss being home for Christmas and New Year's Eve. If you don't bid, you usually get a really tough schedule. He felt terrible about forgetting. I was so sad about it but told him it was okay, we all forget things. That night he spent hours repeating the healing words of ho'oponopono over and over. The next morning the airline called him and said, *"We are so sorry. Our computer system went down last night, and everyone's bids were erased. Do you mind sending in your bid again?"* We both cried. In ten years of his working there, neither of us had ever heard of that happening. He was home for Christmas and New Year's Eve that year.

Miracles happen with this. I've seen it and heard other's stories as well.

For myself, this has been another thing I do to show myself love. When I say the words, I feel them settling into my body. I feel comforted by them.

I use them when I am triggered by something someone said, when fears pop up in my brain, during times I'm feeling sad or angry and don't know why. It's all a chance for me to clear out all that is in me that is ready to leave and be healed.

Throughout our lives, we experience things that end up creating limiting and damaging thoughts in our brains. After a time, many of these thoughts turn into solid beliefs. Most of the time we live our lives unaware of how much these beliefs dictate the way our lives play out.

As we clear out these beliefs and thought patterns that cause us a lot of stress and unhappiness, we are able to be more still and feel our true essence. Our core is filled with peace and unconditional love.

I use this healing method in a very intuitive way. I go with the words I feel like saying. Sometimes all that is needed for me is *"I love you"* or *"I'm sorry"*. Your body knows what it needs.

I hope this was helpful to you. I love sharing things that have worked and continue to work for me.

The core of you is so clean and beautiful. You are so pure. Your body and mind feel best when they live there with your true essence. Anything that causes you to feel pain is not you and is ready to be cleared out.

Much love and kindness to you today as you get closer and closer to the beauty and peace that rests within you.

8

Photo Albums

For years, to-do lists have dominated my days. In some ways, I feel like I have lived my life trying to get through an endless list of things to do with the unspoken hope that one day there will be nothing to do, and then I can rest and just be. It feels like I've been in overdrive for most of my adult life.

A week ago I took off for two days to a retreat center to write. My goal was to write and write and write in this book. I figured that without the distractions of home I would get so much done, so much accomplished. Instead, what happened was not what I had planned.

Whenever I sat in front of my computer screen to write, nothing came. I felt frustrated, discouraged. So I went on walks to clear my head and ended up sitting under trees a lot, stopping at times to sit in the grass because it looked so soft and inviting. Nothing in me wanted to write. I just wanted to be. I just wanted to feel the grass and look up at the sky.

I finally decided to let go of my agenda and just let myself do what I felt like doing. I ended up spending hours hiking up to my favorite rock and just sitting there. Sometimes I sat on a picnic table and stared for a long time. I would lie down on that same table and watch the clouds. At first, I had many thoughts go through my mind, but I eventually noticed the thoughts not coming as often. They became very basic. I began to feel a stillness inside me that felt calming, peaceful. By the end of my time there, my body felt so relaxed. I felt strength, firmness inside the core of me. I didn't feel like talking a lot. I was present without trying to be.

When I got home I wanted to keep this feeling. I was afraid of falling into the to-do list way of living again. But I remembered how good that time was for me, so I looked at my day planner and crossed out whatever I didn't really have to do. I only left essential tasks. I made room for nothingness in my day, as much open time as I could possibly have. I decided to put off goals I saw as important before and now saw as secondary to my new goal of having more time to just be.

I felt some fear that if I didn't pursue things on my to-do list, then my life would not move forward, I would have no life, I would wander aimlessly and accomplish nothing. At the same time, I knew my life would not be fully authentic, it would not be based on the core of me, it would not be an inspired life if I didn't take the time to connect with myself, to listen, to be.

During my first day back home I found myself lying on the living room floor just because I felt like it. After some time lying there, an idea came to me. I loved it and decided to act on it.

I felt prompted to talk to myself at every age, to show myself love. I went downstairs and pulled out a pile of old photo albums.

First I looked at baby pictures. In years past I would look at old photos and feel either the pain or the joy I was feeling at the time. This time my job was to love myself.

Looking at me as a baby brought up so much love, *"Oh my gosh. You are so cute! If you were right here, I would so want to pick you up and hold you!"* I could feel a settling sensation in my body as I continued to say loving things to my young self.

Seeing myself during early school years, I smiled and said, *"I see you. I see that light in your eyes, that zest for life, that adventurer inside you. No matter what you are going through right now, you still have that spark in you. I love that about you, Debbie."*

When I looked at myself in sixth grade, I said, *"Oh Debbie. I can see the light in your eyes has dimmed. This is a hard time for you. I know. I still see that spark, though. It's still there. I love you. Your heart is so tender, and I love that about you. You are so sensitive. That is a powerful trait you have. I love you, sweet Debbie."*

I continued loving myself through many ages and stages of my life. The feeling I felt inside me as I said these words, as I only brought love and acceptance to the table, was profound. It felt like shifts were happening in me; like healing was occurring. My body felt warm, taken care of, nurtured, accepted, embraced. It felt like I kept exhaling sighs of relief. I felt safe. Cared for. More and more the sense settled in that nothing was wrong with me at any age and so much was lovable about me. It all felt incredibly healing and cleansing.

After a while, I began to feel tired and decided to do the other years another time. Listening to what my body needed, I went back upstairs to rest and let the healing that had just occurred continue to integrate with my body.

I was so grateful for the guidance I received on my living room floor that day. We are not alone. There is help we cannot see and in the stillness, in our being-ness, we can feel it.

I hope you take the time to just be when you need to, when you are feeling overwhelmed, uninspired, lost, in need of love and attention. You are worth the time. Being still, connecting with your true self, is some of the most important work you will do in this life. May you feel loads of love, tenderness, and healing today.

9

Healing Your Inner Child

When I am feeling scared or anxious about something in my life, another thing I do that helps me create a safe space is to spend time with my inner child.

For me, this is a meditative process. I close my eyes, take a few deep breaths, focus on my breathing, and begin to see myself as a young girl standing near me. Her age comes intuitively for me. I go with what I see. This is most helpful when I allow the visualization to come instead of trying to make something happen.

I will often ask her, in my mind's eye, if she wants to come sit on my lap and tell me how she is feeling. Sometimes she wants to and other times she doesn't. I respect her wishes, her boundaries. This is a time for me to let her know she is safe here. She can say anything she wants. She won't be judged, only loved. She also has permission to act out in any way she needs to.

Most of the time she sits on my lap. I ask her how she is feeling. I listen. I ask her more questions. If she says she is feeling scared, I ask her to tell me what she is scared of. Then I talk to her.

I tell her I understand and it's okay to feel whatever she feels. Then I talk to her about whatever it is she is afraid of. I remain the mature, wise adult that knows what she needs to hear. I always tell her the truth in a very calm and loving way. I explain to her whatever she doesn't understand. I hold her and let her cry if that's what she needs. I reassure her that everything is going to be okay, and I explain why. I let her know I am always here for her. She never has to go through anything alone.

It's remarkable how I feel my body relax when I do this, even though it's me who is calming myself. I think there is something that wakes up in us when we see a young version of ourselves expressing their fear. We naturally want to take care of them, to be the nurturer they/we need in that moment. I find I instinctively know what to say, what my little self needs to hear and feel.

Another version that is really powerful and can, in fact, change wounding memories for us, is when I replay a painful memory from my life. I freeze the other people in the scene of the memory, like stopping a movie reel, and I walk up to my younger self and speak to her.

For example, when I was four years old I was yelled at in a public place by a significant adult in my life because of something I had done, something very innocent like accidentally spilling something or accidentally breaking an object that wasn't mine. I don't remember exactly what I did, but I remember being yelled at in public and how I felt inside. I'm also aware of how times like these built on each other and shifted the way I see life and myself, affected how I've chosen to live.

I felt shame at that moment. I learned to be quiet and very poised and controlled in life. I grew up trying to be as perfect as I possibly could to avoid being yelled at and feeling the way I did at that moment.

So I closed my eyes and went back to that scene. I saw myself getting yelled at and watched my little self feeling devastated, lost, and alone. I paused everyone else in the scene and walked up to my little self as my now-adult self. I knelt down by her and wrapped my arm around her and said, *"It's okay, Debbie. You didn't know. You didn't mean to do anything wrong. You didn't do anything wrong. You are innocent. You were just being curious. I love that about you. You were excited. It's totally okay. It's totally normal. You don't need to feel bad. I want you to know that this man yelling at you is not okay. He is the one that did something wrong. Not you. Yelling at you is not what love looks like and you deserve love, sweet Debbie. You were made for love, and when someone doesn't treat you with love it doesn't feel good. That's why you are feeling confused right now. I want you to do something. I want you to be really kind to yourself. And if you have any questions, you can always ask me."*

"Why did he yell at me? Why is he so angry?" she asked.

"He is angry because he is scared. He is scared that the man at this market will be mad at him because of what happened. He feels like he needs to do everything perfectly. He doesn't know that it's okay to make a mistake. It's okay to spill things, to accidentally break things. It's normal. He puts a lot of pressure on himself. But you know what? That's okay. He will figure out how to love himself. You don't need to do that for him. You just need to know that who you are is wonderful. Everyone is okay. No one needs to get mad. And if they do, that just means they're scared and, someday, they will figure out they don't need to be. In the meantime, know that you are a pleasure to have around, that I love your excitement for things, your curiosity, and how animated you are. I love you, Debbie. What would you like to do now? What sounds like it would feel really good to do now?"

I share this with you knowing these words are universal truths. Knowing you have had moments in your life that have shaped you, that have made you more cautious, that have added fear to your life that doesn't need to be there. All can be healed, my love. All can be restored.

I hope this is helpful, and I hope you will hold your precious young self when she or he needs to be held, listened to, and guided.

You deserve love, healing, and the freedom to be your full self.

10

Mom

My mom passed away about a year and a half ago. I don't think her presence in my life can ever be filled by anyone else. She was a very special woman.

One thing she often said after listening to me share my heart was, *"I can understand how you would feel that way."*

I loved that sentence because it told me I was accepted, no matter what. My feelings were okay to feel. She may not agree with my thinking, but my heart mattered more than sharing the same opinion. Her words calmed me.

I won the lottery when it came to the mom I was given. She had such a gentle way about her. She asked me about things that were going on in my life and intently listened while saying kind words like *"That's so great, Debbie"* and *"Wow, that's wonderful"*. Her words and the way she delivered them settled in my body like a warm blanket.

The other day, I met and spoke to my friend's mom over

Skype for the first time—or *Mum*, as he calls her. She spoke to me the way my Mom used to. I cried after our call, realizing I don't have a motherly figure in my life anymore and how much I miss that, how much I need those words, that supportive energy. I have great friends and a precious support system I'm incredibly grateful for, but there are times I just want my mom.

If I was going through a difficult time, my mom would stop whatever she was doing to be there for me, to listen, to hold me, to say reassuring things. She was my biggest fan, the most consistent believer in me.

I remember often resting my head on her lap, how she would gently glide her hands through my hair, speaking to me with her naturally soothing voice. My body always relaxed and, somehow, in that moment, I always knew everything was going to be okay. Even when she had dementia and had forgotten most things in her life, her instincts still kicked in when I placed my head on her lap. No memory loss could change who she was at her core.

I felt unconditionally loved by her. When I accidentally broke something in the house, she was more concerned that I didn't feel bad about it than the fact an object in her home was broken.

She told me her greatest joy in life was loving my sister and me.

When I was in high school, she would notice I was tired and stressed out and would say, *"I think you need the day off. Why don't you skip school tomorrow and we can spend the day together?"* The following day she would have me bring a note to school that said, *"Please excuse Debbie's absence. She was absent for health reasons."* She explained to me that health could mean physical, mental, or emotional, so needing a day off from school because I was tired or burned out fell into that category.

We didn't have a lot of extra money growing up. I got a job as soon as I could and paid for my own clothes. One day I told her about a yellow floral dress I saw at T.J.Maxx. I had fallen in love with it but it was thirty-five dollars, which seemed outrageous to me at the time. She wanted to know all about it, every detail.

The next day I came home from school, walked into my room, and lying on my bed was the yellow floral dress. My mom had spent the day scouring through racks and racks of clothes, which is not a simple task in that store, found the dress in my size, and bought it using money I'm sure could have gone to something more needed.

During her last day with us, she was in her home lying in a hospital bed provided by the beautiful people from Hospice. I crawled into bed with her, rested my head on her shoulder, and held her hand for as long as I could. I wanted to feel what it felt like to be next to her for as long as I possibly could before I had to say goodbye.

When I would visit my parents as an adult, my dad told me she always made sure there were grapes in the fridge because she knew I loved them.

When I was a new mom I felt like I didn't know what I was doing, thinking I was blowing it and not doing a good job. She would say wise things like, *"Debbie, they will remember the overall. You will mess up here and there, but they will remember how you loved them overall."*

There are times I need advice, times I need to work through my thoughts and use other coaching tools to help me be free of limiting beliefs and to see clearly. Then there are times I just need a mother's love.

During these times I speak to myself in very nurturing ways, saying things my mom would tell me if she was here.

The other day when I felt like I wasn't handling life well, when I felt "less than", when I was feeling overwhelmed, I took a walk and thought of my mom, and I said things to myself like, *"Debbie, I can understand how you would feel that way. Your plate is very full right now. You are dealing with a lot. So much of this is new to you. I'm so proud of the way you are handling everything. You're going to figure this out. You are amazing and so capable. I'm so impressed with you, honey."*

I could feel the soothing effect these words had on my body. I could feel the warm hug of my mom's arms.

Not all of us had a mom who loved us the way mine did.

If you didn't, I will share mine with you. She would want nothing less.

If you have someone in your life that is like my mom, soak in their love, let yourself feel it.

My mom was not perfect. She would want you to know that. There were many things she didn't do that other moms did. But here is the thing: I remember the overall.

I need to get groceries today. Maybe I'll pick up some grapes.

I hope you can do something for yourself today that a loving mom, or mum, would do for you.

11

Words I Rest In

Only Good Will Come From This

There are times when I am feeling a lot about something that is happening in my life or happening inside me, and I have no idea what to do about it. I don't know how to solve it, and I may not have the energy or motivation or desire to do any "work" on myself. It's in these times that I turn to these words—

Only good will come from this.

There are times I forget I have unseen helpers who love me tremendously and enjoy being here, with me and for me. During these times of feeling lost, I stop and say out loud—

Only good will come from this.

I can feel the words settling into my body, reassuring it that all is well. It feels like a proclamation I am making, and it feels as if it makes it so when I say it. It brings me peace when things around me don't feel like they make sense.

Only good will come from this.

Sometimes I'm tired and don't know where my path is leading me. I don't know what to do next.

Only good will come from this.

Every time I say these words I feel comforted. My body relaxes a bit. I am reminded that I don't need to do anything in this moment. It's okay for me to just be. These words are a reminder to me that everything is going to be okay. Everything is going to work out. All is well.

Only good will come from this.

These words are a comfort, a promise, of sorts. A promise that whatever is happening is happening for a reason.

Only good will come from this.

There is nothing I need to do right now. Nothing I need to change. Nothing I need to fix. Nothing I need to work on.

Only good will come from this.

In times of confusion, times of overwhelm, I give you these words, my love:

Only good will come from this.

12

Spiritual Closet

Most of us hide in different ways. We tone ourselves down for fear of being too much for other people.

Some of us hide our beauty because we are scared of the attention we might get from others. At times we hide how smart we are. There are situations where we keep our political views to ourselves, knowing someone in the group will lose their marbles if they hear who we are really thinking of voting for in the next election.

One way I hide is by not being fully honest about my religious/spiritual beliefs.

I grew up very Christian. And by that, I mean very, very, very Christian.

My parents were missionaries. I went to church every Sunday morning and evening and, when I was a teenager, also Wednesday nights for Awana and youth group. In high school, I also went to different homes on Tuesday nights for weekly meetings put on by an organization called Youth For Christ. I attended their burger bashes, winter retreats, and a trip to Florida over spring break.

I helped organize a prayer group that met every Monday morning at a church across from my high school to pray for all the students in my school. In high school, my best friend and I vowed never to go to any parties that served alcohol. We also made a habit of hiding Ouija boards in stores to protect people from evil. We wanted to be lights in the darkness. I felt burdened for my non-Christian friends and wanted to save as many as I could.

I listened to Christian music ninety percent of the time. My journal wasn't filled with entries about boyfriends or what happened over the weekend. The pages were lined with what my quiet time with God was like that morning. Some were apologies to God for not spending time with Him.

I had questions I wanted to be answered after high school and felt myself leap with excitement when I sat in on the Old Testament Survey class at Moody Bible Institute while visiting a friend. This was the place for me, I decided. My wild college years were spent wearing dresses at Moody, except for Fridays when pants were allowed. My first priority in life was my relationship with God.

I had no idea what I wanted to do with my life, career-wise. I just wanted to get to know God as much as I possibly could.

During my first semester at Moody, I met weekly with one of my professors to go over all the questions I had about the Bible.

I sang in the choir, became a resident assistant, and served on a board deciding if a couple should be kicked out of school for having premarital sex and determining if stretch pants should be outlawed because they caused the male students to stumble (lust).

My friend, Liz, and I used to order pizza, eat it in our rooms, and quietly say swear words to each other, laughing hysterically.

I dated a guy at Moody for about a year and a half. We had strict physical standards. First, we agreed not to kiss until we were engaged—that lasted a few months. Then we said, *"Okay, well, how about if we only kiss standing up so it won't lead to anything else?"* We ended up kissing sitting down, but that's as far as it went.

Being such a dedicated Christian was a mixed bag for me. There were parts I absolutely loved. I felt a connection with God and, when I did, it was the best feeling in the world. I loved having deep talks with other Christians about life and the Bible. I found the Bible fascinating, exciting, and confusing.

I loved stories about angels. I loved the message of unconditional love. I felt the emotions in the Psalms and soaked in the wisdom of Proverbs. I loved stories about Esther and Joseph, as well as Shadrach, Meshach, and Abednego, or as my parents would say at bedtime, *"Shadrach, Meshach, and to bed we go".*

The flip side brought a lot of stress. I felt this pressure to be perfect. I got the message the nice, kind, caring side of me was wanted but not the rest. There were conflicting messages in the Bible I had a hard time getting past, and I was told to just accept and trust God with those.

Probably the most damaging message I got was I couldn't trust myself. In Christianity I was taught we have a carnal nature. That means if we live by our desires, if we make decisions based on our feelings, they could not be trusted because our natural inclination is to sin.

I knew if I was to read things outside the Bible in my search for truth, that would be dangerous territory because I could easily be deceived. All the talk of Satan brought a lot of stress to my body as well. I read verses like:

Be sober-minded; be watchful. Your adversary the devil prowls around like a roaring lion, seeking someone to devour. (1 Peter 5:8) and

But I am afraid that as the serpent deceived Eve by his cunning, your thoughts will be led astray from a sincere and pure devotion to Christ. (2 Corinthians 11:3)

and

Satan disguises himself as an angel of light. (2 Corinthians 11:14)

In my early 30s, I began to be drawn to different types of teachings. When I heard Ellen DeGeneres talk about a new book that had come out called *The Secret,* I was more than intrigued. I went to Barnes & Noble and asked the lady at the Customer Service desk if they had the book. She said, *"Oh, yes. That would be in the New Age section."* My heart sank. She may as well have said, *"Oh, yes, that would be in the Satan section."*

I pretty much parked myself at Barnes for the next two years, reading a massive number of books, exploring ideas that intrigued me. At one point, after reading a book where a woman was channeling an entity named Abraham, I texted Liz, *"It's official. I'm going to hell."* I felt so much fear as I walked deeper down the rabbit hole of ideas that were getting more and more out there.

There was so much fear in me about being led astray. How could I know what the truth is? The only reliable, trustable sources were the Bible and most Christian books and study guides. Anything outside those was dangerous. If the message made me feel good, it might be a trick from the Devil trying to lure me away from God.

The other thing that happens when you leave the confines of Christianity, when you stray from its beliefs and go rogue, is you are no longer trusted by most devout evangelical Christians. They become concerned for you and you become a prayer request at their Bible study groups. The thing that stung the most for me was feeling like I wasn't worth being heard anymore because, in their minds, as the Bible wasn't my main source of truth anymore, whatever thoughts I now had could not be trusted, because I was being influenced by something other than God. That was my experience, anyway.

It felt like in one moment I was no longer part of the tribe that had been my world for most of my life. It was painful. I felt alone.

There is a safety in Christianity that I miss. I miss feeling part of a group, a family. I miss singing in church. I miss knowing for sure what I believe. It's trickier when there is no system to fall back on. Everything was laid out for me in Christianity.

Now my only compass is myself, my feelings, how my body reacts when I hear something. I suppose, when I think about it, that's all people had to go on for centuries before the existence of the Bible. It's easy to forget there was a time when we didn't have a Bible, a Koran, a Book of Mormon. What did people do then? How did they know what was truth?

I have more questions than answers now.

In Western culture, we are so results-driven that wandering over the earth aimlessly isn't valued as a respectable way of living, although I think that mentality is changing.

There is something that feels insecure about not having a belief system, although the longer I am without one, the more interesting and fascinating life is feeling.

I have had more magical experiences, I would say because of not being attached to one way of thinking. That has opened up the world to me, and I notice more than I used to. I notice myself knowing things before they happen. I notice my ability to feel things I can't see. I have had experiences that are out-of-this-world bizarre and exciting.

In my quest to make my body a safe place to reside, this is one area I have been more kind to myself. I've been giving myself permission to not know things. Allowing myself to wander. Not equating my worth with being certain about things.

This has also made me a much more curious and accepting person.

We are all on our individual journeys. Things aren't laid out clearly for any of us if we're really honest. It would be nice if we could all admit that and support each other while we are all doing our best to figure things out.

I recognize there are people who just don't really care. I have friends who water ski in the summer and snow ski in the winter, and deep thoughts about why we are here don't seem to cross their minds. They seem quite content just skiing their way through life. There are times I envy that. But for us deep thinkers, seekers, and wanderers, let us be kind to ourselves and to each other.

It's interesting because I still feel the same feelings I had when I spent time with God as a Christian. I still feel a connection to something I cannot see. It feels like love and acceptance beyond anything I've experienced on this earth. In my mind, this kind of love would never reject me for not knowing something. This love would embrace me and say, *"I'm so proud of you. You are honest, and you seek the truth. You are brave."*

If that deep love comes from God, then I believe he would pursue me with the fierceness of a lion and love me no matter what path I chose. If the love I feel when I am connected to something beyond my human self is any indication of what God is like, we are loved and accepted no matter what.

The way I have loved myself, created a safe place in this area of my life, is by addressing everything that comes up for me with love, compassion, and kindness. I have needed to give myself permission to be on my own road and to have a road that doesn't look like anyone else's. I allow myself to feel fear and confusion at times. If I feel judged by others, I look at what they are triggering in me by asking how I wish they would treat me, knowing that is what my soul is longing for from me. I've learned to be very proud of myself for carving my own path and taking the risk of trusting myself even if those around me disagree. I've learned if they are concerned for me, that comes from their own fear, and I don't need to take that on myself. I can let them own that and I can own my feelings.

Wherever you are in your search, I am with you there. You are not alone. I'm proud of you for asking the difficult questions. I'm proud of you for daring to think for yourself. And I love knowing you are out there.

13

A Powerful Mantra

I was recently watching an interview with Gary Zukav, author of *The Seat of the Soul*. He was asked the question, *"How would you define authentic power?"* His response was something I had never heard before, but when I heard it, it felt profoundly true and wise.

He said, *"There is only one way to be authentic. Only love is authentic. Everything else is not accessing our fullest potential."* I feel the truth of this. When I am deeply connected to myself I feel a profound love in and around me that overpowers everything else.

When I am quiet. When I meditate. When I pray. When I am able to be still and feel my true self, when I am able to be at a place where the chatter in my mind quiets down, I feel love at the center of myself.

This is who we are.

When we are not in this state of love we feel out of sorts, our mind goes nuts playing a distorted commentary on everything that is happening in our lives.

I believe we were made for love, to love, and to be loved, and when that isn't happening, when that's not what we're experiencing, we are filled with unease.

In many ways, living in this world feels strange and foreign to me. I've never truly felt like this is my home; like I fit in here. I tend to trust people, believe the best of them, and when I am lied to, manipulated, or treated badly, my body reacts to it with confusion. In a sense, that behavior feels foreign to me.

There is something in me that has always felt as if I have experienced what it's like to live around love in its purest, truest form, and when I don't experience that here, it feels jarring and physically shocking to my body because it is not used to it, not made for that.

I do experience love here, and I rarely ever take that for granted, or the beautiful people who treat me with kindness. I soak up their love. It's a memory of what home feels like, and I pour my own love on them because it feels most natural to do that. I feel most alive and free when I experience love.

When I am treated badly or I hear about others being treated unkindly, I can physically feel my body being traumatized by it. Anything outside of love feels like it goes against my nature, the core of who I really am.

Do you relate to that? I have a feeling many of you do. When we are really honest with ourselves, there is nothing that heals us and soothes us more than love because we were made for it. It is who we are.

So, what do we do? How can we access our authentic power? What does that look like?

It looks and feels like meeting yourself with love.

The other day I found myself bombarded with fearful thoughts, jealous feelings, anger, and frustration. These feelings usually come in waves for me but there weren't a lot of breaks on this particular day. No ebb and flow, just a continuous nasty, hurtful, overwhelming stream. I kept waiting for the beautiful release of ebb, but it wasn't showing up.

After some time of this, I found myself beginning to meet every feeling, every thought with three words: I love you. To every thought that came to mind that sent me spiraling, I said, *"I love you."* Instead of trying to change my thoughts or distract myself or make some kind of plan, I just kept meeting myself with love, and each time I did I felt my body sink down and relax a little more.

Deep down I knew that behind all the unhelpful and hurtful words coming to mind there was fear. That's all. A little girl in me was afraid and the one thing she needed more than anything else was love. I could try to reason with her, but her fears go deep, and the most powerful thing that can melt away fear is love.

As my body relaxed more each time I met myself with love, I felt more powerful because I was walking myself out of darkness. The circumstances I thought would bring me relief weren't changing, my inner compass was. My fearful thoughts no longer had power over me.

When we walk with love as the core of us we are grounded and unaffected by things that happen to us, hurtful words that are spoken to us, and circumstances that might otherwise have thrown us into panic and fear. When we walk in love there is strength and a steadiness that is with us through all things. There is more of a knowing of who we are, bringing us a more solid sense of self that isn't swayed by other negative opinions of us.

As you move through your day, I hope you meet yourself with love. You were made for this. It is who you are, and it is what will heal, free, and empower you.

14

No Judgment

"I should have eaten better today."

No judgment, Debbie.

"I should be better with money... I should be saving more."

No judgment, Debbie.

"I make so many bad decisions with money."

No judgment, Debbie.

"I feel overwhelmed and wish I could handle life better."

No judgment, Debbie.

Lying on the hammock in my backyard, staring at the sky, I started to list all the things I was feeling discouraged about.

After every statement I made, the sentence kept coming—

"I just feel like I can't get it together."

No judgment, Debbie.

"I still don't know what career I want to have. I feel like I waste so much time."

No judgment, Debbie.

I just let it all come. All the things I berate myself for.

It felt meditative. Whenever I said the words "No judgment", especially followed by my name, it was like a kind soul was next to me, holding my hand and leading me down a path of unconditional, calming love.

"Why am I not more motivated in life?"

No judgment, Debbie.

I felt my body being able to exhale more, feeling calmer, more at ease.

"Other people seem to know how to do this life. After all these years, I still feel like I don't know what I'm doing."

No judgment, Debbie.

"Am I just going to wander for the rest of my life?"

No judgment, Debbie.

"I wish I could stick to something like meditation, exercise, finishing this book. Will this book be yet another thing in my life that I talk about and don't finish?

No judgment, Debbie.

The more I responded with that, the more I noticed the fearful words I was saying starting to become chatter, noise that just didn't matter to me anymore. My body feeling calm and soothed became the only thing that mattered.

Whatever stressful thoughts you are having about yourself right now, I hope you give yourself the gift of no judgment today.

You don't need to do anything to prove anything. I love you. May you be well. May you live your life with ease. May you know you are enough just the way you are.

No judgment.

15

Mirror Work

Years ago I read about *mirror work* in one of Louise Hay's books. I have tried saying different things to myself with different goals in mind throughout the years, and I have discovered a healing method that has been incredibly powerful and effective for me.

Louise said to look in a mirror and say, *"I love and approve of myself."* I felt disheartened when I first tried this years ago because I found it quite difficult to do. It's a vulnerable thing to face your own eyes looking back at you.

My daughter walked in the room while I was holding up the mirror. She was around eight years old at the time. I explained the exercise I was doing and asked her if she wanted to try. She playfully snapped up the mirror, smiled, and with all the confidence in the world she had no problem saying, *"I love and approve of myself!"*

I was amazed at how easy it was for her. She didn't blink an eye. She jumped right in. This gave me hope. I had more years of built up insecurities and unkind beliefs about myself, but there was something about seeing how possible it was that encouraged me to keep going with it.

I felt uncomfortable saying things to myself I didn't fully believe, so I started with baby steps. Instead of saying *"I love and approve of myself"* I would look into my eyes and say, *"I want to love and approve of myself."* After some time of doing this, I came to a place where I could honestly say, *"I love and approve of myself".*

Over the years, what I say while looking into my eyes has evolved into a deep inner healing process.

It has become a conversation between the scared and unsure part of myself and a higher me who is fully aware of the truth of my value.

I start out by holding up the mirror, looking into my eyes, and noticing what comes up for me. I might begin by saying, *"I love you."*

I may notice fear in my eyes and gently say, *"I see your fear... It's okay... What are you afraid of?"*

I'll wait for an answer.

Being bored in life. Endlessly wandering.

I'll keep listening for anything that needs to be voiced.

I'm scared of things not working out. I'm scared of being alone and feeling lost. I'm scared of not having enough money.

"*Ok… I hear you. I see you. What else? What else are you afraid of?*"

I'm scared you won't take care of me.

"*Mmmm… What else?*"

I'm scared I'm going to always be tired and never get to a place where I feel good about how I eat and exercise.

I can feel tension building in me at this point. I decide just to be with myself and look deeper into my eyes. This is a very intuitive process. I go with what I feel I need.

"*I love you,*" I say again as I continue to look into my eyes. I start to cry and just let the tears come. "*It's okay… I know… I'm so proud of you,*" I tell myself as I cry. I keep looking into my eyes, "*I know you're scared. It's okay. You cry as long as you need to. I'm still here. I'm not going anywhere… You're beautiful when you cry. Do you know that? You're full of passion and feeling, which is so lovely and drawing. I love you.*"

Oftentimes I don't feel like explaining anything to that scared part of me. I don't feel like coaching her or giving her any advice. I sense that she just needs to be heard. After some time I feel my body start to relax. I feel loved. I feel heard. I feel seen. I trust myself more. Just showing up and staying with my fears feels powerfully healing.

As I write this, I think of you. I get so much joy from thinking of you doing this for yourself if it draws you, from thinking of this kind of love and personal heart attention spreading throughout the world. How powerful that would be.

The more you do this, if you choose to, the more you will develop your own way, your own personal rhythm. Your body will relax, and a peaceful knowing that everything is going to be okay will settle in.

Much love and compassion to you today, dear reader.

16

What Do I Wish They Would Do?

Over the years I've been made aware of the concept that, in many ways, we are mirrors of each other. This can feel painful and frustrating when we are triggered by other's behavior but, most importantly, this is a huge gift and a blessing. It is here to help us heal and to be free. It is our soul reaching out.

For instance, if someone treats me in a way that causes me to feel hurt or angry, they are reflecting something within me that is ready to come up and be healed. When this happens, I have learned to ask myself these questions: *"What do I wish they would do? What do I wish they would say? What would feel really good for them to do? How do I wish they would behave?"*

Whatever the answers are, those are what my soul is wanting from me. They are what I need to give myself.

In many ways, what we are feeling has nothing to do with the other person. They are a vehicle to help us heal the parts of ourselves that need to be loved.

As an example, someone might give me unsolicited advice

on what I should be doing with my life. That feels irritating to me.

When I notice this upsetting me, I know something is being triggered in me that is ready to be healed. So I ask myself, *"What do I wish they would say to me? How would I like them to treat me? What would feel good?"* This becomes a meditative time for me to go within and get in touch with what I am longing for.

My answer is, *"It would feel so good if they said, 'Debbie, I so trust you. I believe you are going to create such an amazing life. Keep trusting yourself. Everything is going to work out for you. I can't wait to see what you end up creating, the life you will end up living. It's going to be amazing because you are amazing. I have no doubts that you will find a way to live a life that fits you and supports you beautifully.'"*

When I realize this is what I am longing to hear, then I know this is what my soul is wanting from me—to trust and believe in myself. I have fears around not being able to support myself through doing things I love, and my body, my heart, every part of me is asking me to trust.

When I do this I am no longer a victim of someone else's words or approach. I am back in charge of me. Now I have the knowledge I need to know how to love myself.

Whenever I get in touch with this, the words I hear coming out of myself always feel calming. Truth feels that way. Love feels that way in our bodies.

It can start with a brief encounter with a grumpy person in a store, a comment said on social media, a text message, a conversation with a family member, or even a well-meaning friend. Anything that gets a rise out of us is worth looking at. It's here to help us. Everything is, really.

When I get to what it is my soul wants from me, I do different things depending on what I feel drawn to. Sometimes I do *ho'oponopono*, sometimes mirror work, other times I just acknowledge what I'm feeling and remind myself I'm still here. Tears might come. I may feel the need to just talk to myself in a very loving and affirming way, to say things my mom would have said to me. Whatever feels needed and good at that moment is what I do.

It's amazing how my attitude toward the person changes after I do this. Sometimes I feel more tender toward them, realizing they have their own fear, anger, or sadness that made them act the way they did. If they've had a hold over me, the way a bully does, they begin to feel smaller and sometimes nonexistent. They just naturally leave the space in my head they used to occupy. The power they had over me lessens.

Every experience we have, every reaction we feel, is here to serve us. We have the power to heal ourselves. And because we are also a mirror to others, in turn, we help heal those around us by loving ourselves.

In many ways, every experience we have here on earth is sacred and filled with love. We are being pursued, courted by our soul from the most loving place possible.

17

What Love Looks Like

For about a year before my divorce was final, the interactions I had with my husband felt extremely confusing to me. He would say things that sounded like they could be right, he spoke with authority and confidence, but when he spoke my body felt weak. I felt all jumbled inside. I couldn't think clearly. I questioned my own thoughts and reactions. He seemed to know what he was talking about. He appeared to be clear in his thinking whereas I felt like a mess so, in my mind, that meant I couldn't trust myself. He must know more than me because I don't feel clear. People who seem to be confident can appear right.

His words sounded rational, but inside I wanted to scream. Sometimes his sentences appeared kind, other times they ripped through me like an unforgiving blade. He said things about me that didn't sound like me, but I wondered if maybe he knew me more than I knew myself.

I lived in a puddle of confusion and tears for a long time, trying to see clearly. I turned to family and friends who had known me for a long time to help me see what was happening. I went to counseling. Most days I didn't want to get out of bed.

Then one day I was at a store and saw a canvas hanging on the wall. It was lined with words from 1 Corinthians 13 in the Bible:

> *Love is patient, love is kind. It does not envy, it does not boast, it is not proud. It does not dishonor others, it is not self-seeking, it is not easily angered, it keeps no record of wrongs. Love does not delight in evil but rejoices with the truth. It always protects, always trusts, always hopes, always perseveres.*

I couldn't take my eyes off those words. It was like seeing water after months of wandering the desert. I promptly bought the wall hanging and put it in my bedroom. I would sit and stare at it for long periods of time. It became a lifeline for me. I needed to be reminded of what love looks like and feels like. It helped me see what I was experiencing fell far short of the real thing. The truth of those words helped me trust myself more, trust that my physical and emotional reactions were there for a reason.

We are made for love, and when we are not experiencing the real thing, our bodies react. It doesn't feel good when it is treated with something other than love.

It's an incredibly beautiful thing, the way we are made. Our body feels alive, free, safe, and relaxed when love is being presented. We feel valued, heard, and fully accepted.

If we are feeling tightness, weakness, confused, unsettled, deflated, sad, uncomfortable, angry, or like there is something wrong with us, we are not experiencing love from either ourselves or others.

When we are being treated with love, we feel calm, reassured, good about ourselves, connected with the world around us, at peace, hopeful, and feel love for others and ourselves.

For most of my life, I developed the pattern of taking the blame for things that were not my fault or my issue. I have experienced men in my life that didn't own up to their issues; instead, they projected them onto me, and I took the blame. I, of course, was not aware of this dance that was happening for most of my life.

Because of this, I have ended up feeling like things were wrong with me when the reality was I was fine. I was being mistreated and not noticing it because it was so subtle. No one was hitting me, yelling at me, saying mean things to me. These men were more passive in their aggression. Like stealth bullies that fly below the radar and go unnoticed by most.

I do want to say, as a side note, I am not against men. In fact, I love men who are honest and kind. I have some great male friendships that are beautiful. I wouldn't want to live in a world without them. When a man is authentic, tender, takes personal responsibility, has a strong sense of self, and comes from a place of love, that is a powerful and much-needed force in this world.

It's incredibly helpful to have friends who treat us with love.

Liz and I have been friends for over thirty years. In all that time she has never said anything that put me down. I feel completely safe with her. I know I can be fully honest with her. She loves and accepts me just the way I am. She enjoys me. She sees me as a gift in her life. I don't think I have ever been afraid to talk to her about anything. I have never felt jumbled inside when talking to her, never felt weak. I notice I like who I am when I am with her.

My friend Sonja values what I say, doesn't look at me as flawed but as powerful. She sees my beauty when I am not able to and lets me know the essence she sees and feels in me. I feel free to be completely honest with her about all my fears, all my longings. She finds me to be refreshing and would never want to change anything about me. I feel emotionally safe with her.

I give you these examples as a reference point because we need them. We need to be reminded of what love looks like and feels like.

The more I treat myself with love and respect, the more I find myself naturally surrounded by people who treat me that way. I notice my body not being able to physically tolerate anything less than love.

The biggest sign for me that something is off is how my body feels around a person. If I find myself recoiling when I am around them, feeling like I need to change something about myself to be wanted, hiding who I really am, feeling sick in any way, I know I am clearly not experiencing love.

When this happens, I do take personal responsibility and look at what is being triggered within me. It helps me know where I need to love myself. Then I become very selective as to who I spend my time with.

I may ask myself, *"Is this a relationship worth investing in, or is it too toxic and I need not be around this person as a way of protecting my heart? Is this someone I need to stand up to or let go of and heal on my own?"*

Have you experienced real love in this life? If not, please use my examples, the verses, touching stories you read, and scenes in movies that feel good to your body as reference points.

Who do you feel the most relaxed around, the most at ease with?

May you feel love today. May you know that you deserve to be loved in its purest form. May you experience love in a way that changes you from the inside out, that reminds you how beautiful and wanted you are. May you be able to recognize when something isn't love and choose to love yourself. May you have the strength to walk away when you need to, as well as the courage to walk toward the real thing when it comes your way.

18

I'm Still Here

I was watching *Dancing with the Stars* yesterday. Paula Deen emotionally broke down during rehearsal. She was tired, unable to focus, afraid her partner would give up on her. Through her tears, she said to him, *"I've been abandoned before, many times."* He tried to reassure her that he would never give up on her. *"I've been abandoned a lot,"* she said. Her sweet and lovely partner, Louis, responded with strength and firmness in his voice, *"Not this time."*

This morning I was praying, asking for divine help with different things. I asked for help with letting go of hurts. I listed discouraging beliefs I had about life and myself and asked for help letting those go. Tears came as I listed different things. As emotions came up in me, I would stop and say to myself, *"I'm here. I'm still here."*

I say this often. It helps me stay in my body, stay present with myself.

This has become a deep practice for me lately. When I am feeling sad, fearful, or anxious, I often stop, close my eyes, and repeat, *"I'm here... I'm here... It's okay... I'm still here."* I say this slowly, meditatively. With each *"I'm here",* I feel my body settling down.

It feels comforting. I can feel myself relaxing, feeling reassured, safe.

It feels like there is a scared child within me that needs reassurance.

The little girl within me needs assurance when strong emotions come up. She needs to know I will stay with her. I will listen without judgment. I am not here to try to change her. I am here to love her. I am her dancing partner. We are in this dance together, and my job is to give her permission to fall apart whenever she needs to and to remind her that I'm not going to abandon her. I am still here.

We need to know we are safe to feel any feeling, at any moment.

Many of us have the belief that if we really let out everything we think and feel, people won't want to be around us. They will leave. We believe we drive others away. Because of things we experienced in life, wounds that occurred, we develop a belief that we are too much to handle.

That's why it is imperative we give ourselves the safe space we need to let our full selves out. We need to reassure ourselves that every part of us is welcome. Every thought, every fear, every feeling is valuable. We are not too much.

The more we choose to stay in our bodies, to be here, to remain present, the more trust is built and the safer we feel.

The next time you feel fear or sadness or anxiety, I hope you remind yourself you are still here and you are not going anywhere. You are here to listen, to love, and to embrace every part of you. You are worth the time, worth the love. You deserve nothing less. You were made for this.

19

The Gift of Depression

Depression is the closest conditioned state to the awakened state.
Chögyam Trungpa Rinpoche

I experienced depression for the first time in my twenties and have been experiencing it quite profoundly over the last few months. This time I have stayed with my feelings, my state of being, instead of seeing it as something that is wrong with me, something that needs to be fixed. Approaching it this way has brought about life-changing results.

I'm noticing I am more present more often, more in my body, and have been experiencing more peace and trust. I have reached the place of not wanting to be here on earth anymore quite a few times, but I knew I wouldn't end my life. I have two kids, and even though I was caring less and less about everything else, I still felt a responsibility to stick around for them.

In my depressed states, I had no desire to engage with this world anymore. Nothing felt exciting. There were no dreams I wanted to go after. I am normally one who creates vision boards, writes out what I want my life to look like, goes after things that light me up. But during these low times, thoughts of those things don't create a spark in me.

There are different types of depression. Sometimes it never lifts, while other times—like for me lately—I go in and out of it. We label depression in different ways. I find it more helpful to drop the labels and just feel what I feel. I think when we have labels attached it can cause more fear and anxiety in us.

When I do decide to sit with it, not judge it, not see it as bad, it feels like a needed time of hibernation for my soul. A time to go within. To comfort myself, to be, to settle in.

From Reginald A. Ray in *Darkness Before Dawn*:

If we take depression as something to be explored, we begin to find that there are a lot of subtleties within it. If we can let go of the idea that we're depressed and simply take depression as an energy or a neutral manifestation of our life, then there's a real journey there for us.

By staying with the feeling, the energy of the depression, I feel in my body that I am wrapping my arms around it, in a sense. I am nurturing something wounded in me, being with something that wants to be heard and needs to be met with love. I let the tears flow when they come. I give it space. You know how good it feels when someone gives you their undivided attention, sits with you and really hears you? It calms you. That's how I feel when I do this for myself. It's giving myself permission to be where I am at this moment. When I do this, it feels comforting, it feels like I am wrapping a warm blanket around myself, lighting a fire, bringing myself tea, and saying, *"What else, Debbie? Tell me everything. I'm here. I'm not going anywhere."*

From this place, everything feels genuine, honest, and there is a peace that comes with that.

I have noticed the more I have been in these states of depression and treated myself this way, the more this feeling of being in my body, being present, is becoming a way of life for me, even after the feelings lift. I like the feeling of being here with myself so much that it's now becoming a way of being for me. It's flowing into every part of my life. I feel more attentive to what is going on inside me and therefore am fully here more than I used to be. When I feel good, it feels more colorful and full-bodied than it used to.

I feel more of a sense of flow happening in and around me. More of a harmonious union with the universe, a trust of myself and everything around me. I feel more of a calm state of being and notice I am more able to love, forgive, and let go of things and people that have wounded me in the past. When I am in this state, everything and everyone around me feel more peaceful. I get the sense I don't need anything from anyone else to fill me. I already have all I need inside myself to feel whole and at peace.

Depression has become my friend in a surprising way, leading me to a much different way of living. A more attentive, kind, gentle way of being.

I think not fearing it anymore has freed me and relaxed me. Seeing the good it brings makes me okay with the times I slide into those feelings.

"Thank you," I find myself saying often, *"Thank you."*

When you can see depression for the gift is actually is, it will open you up to a whole new world where you will experience less fear, more openness and acceptance of self and all that comes with being human.

Much love, peace, and freedom to you today, dear reader. I love you more than either of us could imagine.

20

Aftermath

My kids and I just spent a few beautiful weeks in South Africa. We joined my dad, my sister, and her family, as well as some cousins who live there, to honor my mom's life. She grew up in Swaziland, and none of us had ever seen the land she loved and talked so much about. Our time was filled with love, adventure, and open, heartfelt conversations. We bonded so deeply by the end it was difficult to say goodbye.

On our way home I received an email from my landlord informing me that about one hundred teenagers had a party in our house while we were gone and the police came out to break up the party. My daughter, who had been scared to tell me, said she had given two of her friends permission to spend one night at our house while we were gone. What started as a couple of teens ended up with our address on Twitter and Facebook.

The three of us were scared to see what we would find when we got home. We all spent time cleaning our rooms before we left, knowing how nice it is to come back to a tidy home and to crawl into our comfy beds with crisp, clean sheets after a long journey home. I had scoured the bathrooms, cleared off and wiped down the shelves in the fridge. Dishes were done and put away. Carpets were vacuumed. The home felt great when we left for our trip.

We love traveling, and we love coming back to our home. Our home means a lot to the three of us. I filled it with furniture and placed things on the walls that have meaning, creating a space that feels warm and inviting. It's a relaxing home that feels like a refuge. We've lived in several homes, but this one feels uniquely special.

It is a quiet, peaceful home with nature all around us. When people visit they comment on how relaxed they feel here.

As soon as we walked in, the house felt different. The air felt stagnant, dark, and filled with an unsettled disturbing feeling. The home felt like it had been violated.

Some of the teens had crawled through window screens to get in. A window screen was missing and two others were damaged. There were bottles all over the lawn, stains on the carpets. It smelled like cigarette smoke and weed. Lines of cocaine were found spread out on the desk in my room. There were stains on my son's mattress as well as on the couches in the living room and family room. Weapons were found at the party. Several items were stolen and some things were damaged. Money my kids had saved for years was gone.

We walked around slowly, taking it all in.

Did they take photos of our social security cards? I wondered. *Did they get all my bank information from the files in the office? Are they going to steal my identity from all the info lying around? Did they look through the personal journals in my drawers?*

I got to my room and looked at the shabby chic pink pillows on my bed that look so feminine, so innocent, and I burst out crying. I had visions of all the things that might have gone on next to, and on, my sweet pillows. My bed! I love my bed so much. It has been a place of refuge for me over this last year.

The toilets held remnants of vomit and pee. The floors were sticky. I felt grossed out just walking around. *What had happened on these floors? What am I walking on?*

I pulled the sheets off my bed to wash them. After thirty-five hours of traveling, we were exhausted.

After putting a clean pillowcase on my pillow, I lay down on the bare mattress and breathed in a horrid smell from my pillow. I leaped out of bed. It felt like nothing was safe to touch.

Everything felt defiled. I felt so angry. We all did.

How could people do this?! Have no respect for someone's property, no thought of how this might affect us?

We all felt vulnerable, too. There was a new fear in us, knowing criminals now knew where we live, what we have, how to get in. Would they come back for more? It helped that the locks had been changed and the garage code was different, but still. My daughter slept with me that night after we kept hearing sounds outside.

I woke up the next morning wondering why this happened. I believe things happen for a reason, and this was no exception. I knew good would come from this – I just couldn't see how.

I knew this too would pass. We would get this place cleaned up. We would clear the space emotionally and spiritually. The home would one day feel safe again. I would do what it took to get it there again. It would be a lot of work, a lot of time, but the home would one day feel like a safe refuge again. But in that moment, it was all so overwhelming.

Then a thought came to me as I looked around the house. Everything I was looking at was a picture, a stunning metaphor.

I believe we all come into this life good, pure, innocent. A baby loves to laugh, is naturally curious, dances and cries without any inhibitions. They don't have any thoughts of not being good enough. They soak up love and freely trust those they are around.

We all start out this way. Then living in this world, we experience things early on that affect the way we feel. People come into our lives, just like people came into my home, and defile our sense of safety. As we grow up, more and more people enter our lives. Some wound us with their words. Some take things from us that leave us feeling depleted and scared. We no longer feel like that carefree child who trusted the world, who felt completely free to be themselves.

We start to walk through the world more tentatively, more cautiously, not feeling like we can completely relax when we sit or lie down. Our mind races at all the new anxieties that now reside in us.

When we realize this there is a natural grieving process that occurs, and then a rebuilding and restoring to our original self.

In the morning, after letting more tears come, I was ready to heal this home, to restore it to its original innocence and safety.

Cleaning the toilet that morning became a spiritual experience for me. I didn't use the toxic-free cleaners. I reached for the bleach.

As I spread the cleanser with a cloth, I started to feel the pain of the teens that were here. They had their own arrows that brought them to where they are today, to behave the way they did. I felt a connection with them.

"I'm sorry. Please forgive me. I love you. Thank you," I said over and over with every wipe of every surface of that bathroom.

The cleaning of the house, its restoration, had begun, and I was beginning to see how it would change me in the process too.

I asked the two friends of my daughter's to come over that day to help us clean—I'll call them Ashley and Emma. I also wanted to talk to them about what happened.

I wasn't sure what I wanted to say to them. I was still feeling some anger toward them. I had also heard from my daughter they were really scared to talk to me.

As they walked to the front door hand in hand, I could feel the tension in their bodies. Seeing their fear softened my heart. When I opened the door, all I wanted to do was hold them. They burst out crying as I wrapped my arms around them. Ashley, shaking, said, *"I don't want to let go."* I held onto her for a long time. It felt healing for both of us.

We sat down and they told me the whole story. The girls had invited a few friends who invited more friends, who then put our address on Facebook and Twitter. People they didn't know started showing up. They felt scared and overwhelmed as the house filled up so quickly. One guy came to the door and Ashley told him he couldn't come in. He lifted up his shirt, revealing a knife, and said, *"Yes, I can."* People called her a bitch when she was trying to get them to leave. She ended up sitting on the floor in the corner crying. Finally, the police came after one of the neighbors complained about all the cars.

After hearing all that the girls had to say, it was clear to me they had learned their lesson and were willing to do what it took to make it right. It was also clear to me they had been through their own trauma in this house. There were lots of tears. They felt terrible about what they had done.

When they were done, I didn't feel like being hard on them. All I wanted to do was love them. I told them I had a story I wanted to share with them. I said, *"There is an African tribe that has a tradition. When someone in the tribe does something harmful, they take that person to the center of the village where the whole tribe comes and surrounds them. For two days they say to the person all the good things that he or she has done.*

"The tribe believes that each human being comes into the world as good. Each one of us is only desiring safety, love, peace, and happiness. But sometimes in the pursuit of these things people make mistakes. The community sees those mistakes as a cry for help.

"They unite to lift him or her up, to reconnect them with their true nature, to remind them who they really are until the person fully remembers the truth from which they had been temporarily disconnected: I am good.

"Right now I feel like being that tribe for you," I said, and then told them all the things I thought they were doing well.

It felt good for me to love them. Somehow, embracing the girls felt like I was being held and loved as well. It felt healing for all of us.

It would take time and effort to clean the house and restore it to its original feeling. The same is true for us. It helps to recognize what has happened inside each of us over time. Because of the arrows that have affected our hearts over the years, we all behave in ways that are hurtful to ourselves and others and, more than ever, we need to surround ourselves with and remind ourselves of all the good we do, remind ourselves of who we are. It brings us back to our core, our beautiful, good, loving, pure selves.

If you don't have a tribe who can help remind you, I hope you can remind yourself today. It's a powerful step in the healing process of rebuilding the home inside you. There is healing to be done, a clearing out of all the things that make you feel unsafe. Much love to you on your journey as you reconnect and heal.

You will one day look around inside yourself and realize you feel safe here again. All is well.

21

Forgiveness

At the end of his talk, someone from the audience asked the Dalai Lama, *"Why didn't you fight back against the Chinese?"* The Dalai Lama looked down, swung his feet just a bit, then looked back up at us and said with a gentle smile, *"Well, war is obsolete, you know."* Then after a few moments, his face grave, he said, *"Of course the mind can rationalize fighting back ... but the heart, the heart would never understand. Then you would be divided in yourself, the heart and the mind, and the war would be inside you."*

I've heard several definitions and opinions on the topic of forgiveness. When you don't forgive it's like drinking your own poison. It's not about the other person. It's not accepting the other's behavior; it's a letting go. It's a decision you choose to make.

We can put a lot of pressure on ourselves to forgive someone. It can feel like something we force ourselves to do because we believe we should, or because we've heard it's good for us.

I don't know if it has ever been really clear to me what forgiveness actually is. I've asked many people what they think it is, and their answers go in all directions and never really satisfy the core of me. It feels like there is something we are missing.

There are people who hurt us in smaller ways, like with a hurtful comment. Then there are others in our lives who have wounded our hearts over our entire childhood or most of our adult life. Then there are the ones who have done unspeakable, horrific acts of violence against us, or people we love that we can't imagine ever being able to forgive. Thinking about what they did makes us feel sick, and we can't imagine letting that person off the hook—which is sometimes how the idea of forgiveness feels.

Thinking about what people have done to us or others we love brings up so much anger inside us. It feels violent in our bodies. We feel angry, violated, betrayed, so wronged. The truth is, we were. It was not okay. Any treatment of anyone that is not love is trauma, and our body feels it.

So what do we do with that? We know that keeping all those emotions stored inside us is unhealthy and damaging. We know that, even though a lot of times these people aren't in our lives anymore, we are still feeling the effects of them. Even when we can clearly see it was their issue we are still experiencing trauma, even though the hurtful act(s) is over. But what can we do to not have this happen?

First, we need to let ourselves feel whatever emotions come up around the hurt we have experienced. We must love and accept all of our feelings because they are a part of us. Our bodies were assaulted either physically or emotionally—or both—by someone else. The thing we don't want to do is treat ourselves the same way by not being kind and absolutely accepting of every part of us. We need love and kindness from ourselves more than ever.

I believe our true nature is peace. We are meant to live in a world where love, kindness, respect, and support come as naturally as breathing.

The act of trying to forgive oftentimes feels forced. It's like when we try to be grateful when we are feeling angry or when we try to calm down and say something nice when we really want to scream.

I've learned that if I'm trying to force something, it's either not ready to happen or I'm missing something, a piece to the puzzle.

We push ourselves to do a lot of things. We push ourselves to exercise when we'd rather take a nap. We push ourselves in our careers. We make ourselves talk to others when, if we were honest with ourselves, we would rather not. We force ourselves to do things like yoga because we believe it will bring us more peace, even though our body loathes how it feels.

Trying to forgive someone can have that same energy and is really adding more violence to ourselves.

I believe the key to forgiveness begins with getting really quiet inside ourselves. Being with our Self. Staying there. Letting the tears come, then going deeper into the stillness, the quiet inside of us.

Your body will start to calm itself. You will feel more and more slowed down. You will feel a settling into who you really are, into what you know. You will get in touch with the deep consciousness within you that knows who you are and how life is supposed to feel.

The more you are able to be here and to stay here, the more you will begin to feel what forgiveness feels like, the energy of it. You will feel separated from the pain. It will begin to feel foreign to you. The anger you felt before will begin to disappear naturally. The attachment to the person who hurt you will not be there. You will feel whole in yourself, with yourself.

The more you are able to stay in this space, the deeper you will be able to go within it. The more you are able to feel peace when you are here, the more you will know what home feels like.

When you are home, the idea of forcing anything won't enter your consciousness. When you are home, the idea of feeling angry at someone else doesn't exist. You don't feel the need to forgive anyone. The idea of forgiveness just isn't a concept in your being. It no longer feels necessary.

The feeling of that natural state of love and peace becomes a gentle wave you feel inside you and all around you. This is where you find yourself. This is you at your natural state. This is home.

22

Reconnecting with Your Soul

A few weeks ago, I was having a conversation with a close friend of mine about spirituality. After our talk, I broke down and cried. I realized how disconnected from my soul I was. I had been stressed about a variety of things. My head had been spinning for a while, telling stories that brought up so many fears for me. I had been looking for approval from others and had been out of my body for a while. I had lost myself in the dramas of life.

In that moment, I realized underneath all I had been feeling, my main stress—my sorrow really—was not being connected to my soul, to my true identity. When I speak of "my soul" I am talking about that part of me I feel in meditation or when I am by the ocean, the part of me that feels like pure love and peace. That solid presence that knows who I am and why I am here. The real me. The higher me that holds the scared, unaware me, feeling only love.

I have felt my soul for a very long time. It has always given me the message I am here to help in some way; I am here on earth for a reason. It feels purpose-filled, strong, solid, unwavering.

In the days following that phone conversation, I found myself wanting to retreat from people, from noise. I stopped things I had been doing and listened to what I was longing for, what I needed. I felt like putting everything on hold. My number one priority was to reconnect with my soul, my true self.

The next few mornings I found myself climbing the same mountain. I live in Colorado and am lucky to be quite close to beautiful hikes. I found myself hiking up Spruce Mountain each day because it took the shortest time to get to the top. I just wanted to get to the top and sit there for as long as I needed. I found a spot with lots of signs that said: Do Not Enter. Perfect. There wouldn't be any people there. So every morning I scaled the rocky area, passing the warning signs to the top corner of the mountain that had a breathtaking view. Stuffed in my backpack were my journal, a book, a pen, water bottles, almonds with raisins, and a blanket.

I had no rules for myself. I went with whatever I felt like doing in each moment. I just wanted to be with myself, reconnect. Sometimes I meditated. At times I just stared. I lay down on the blanket and read. I watched birds. I got irritated with flies. Then I let out everything I was feeling. I yelled at angels, God, whoever my unseen helpers were that I felt around me. I told them everything I was feeling, every fear, every reason I thought I was angry. I cried. And sometimes I just got tired of feeling and ate the almonds.

There were times I just lay down on the blanket and felt the warmth of the sun. Sometimes I'd feel frustrated and say, *"I'm here. So, now what? How do I connect with you?"* I tried to be as honest as I could. I refrained from trying to be positive and mature. I let out the scared, most honest part of me. Some of what I let out was the fact I just didn't want to be here anymore. I was over it. The whole thing. Life. Trying. Seeking. It just didn't feel worth it anymore. All the striving. I knew I wouldn't act on it, but my drive to make this life work, to create a life I love, to keep working on myself, to figure out what to do with my life, was just gone. I just didn't care anymore. I didn't care about achieving things anymore, about weight loss, about eating better, about money, about self-help books.

There was something that felt really good about being that honest. It felt like a relief. And in many ways, the not-caring felt like letting go. Stripping myself of all the noise, all the efforts, all the things outside of myself I had made so important. I was left with just me.

On the third day, I was walking back down the mountain and things felt different. I found myself walking at an unusually slow pace. I had no desire to walk fast. As I walked, it felt like I was in a dream. I felt connected to every tree I passed. In fact, I would say I felt in love with every tree I gently glided by. I found myself stopping often, putting my hand on a tree, leaning my head on it like I used to on my mom's shoulder. The trees felt alive to me and full of love. I was struck by the beauty of every part of their trunks, their branches, their leaves. Almost overwhelmed by how stunning they were. I couldn't take my eyes off them.

The trail that had become familiar to me started to feel like an enchanted forest. I felt like I was in a Disney movie and everything around me was a friend. The trees could have gotten together and sewn me a dress or carried me off to some magical place. I wasn't trying to feel this way, it was just happening.

As I entered an open field, a large bird flew overhead, and I felt my body join it. I felt like I was flying with it, connected to it, one with it. I could feel what it felt like to fly. It felt amazing. My body felt like it was being lifted up with it.

As I looked around, the green of the foliage looked like a deeper color than I normally saw, the sky a striking blue. The colors of everything around me were so sharp and crisp. It almost didn't seem real.

I felt alive inside. I was alone and had been feeling a lot of loneliness, but on that trail, at that moment, I didn't feel alone. I felt surrounded by friends, filled with a deep connection that, on a certain level, felt familiar to me.

I'm not exactly sure what led me to that state, what things came together to make that happen in me. I think maybe the combination of showing up, being fully honest, and not running from myself did something. The release of my emotions began a shift in me and invited something in and around me to happen. I felt a commitment to stay with myself, not to run, not to try to be somewhere inside that I wasn't. I think powerful things happen in and around us when we stay right where we are.

There is fear that comes up for a lot of us when we think about being with ourselves, being with our feelings, just listening to them, not trying to change anything. But the truth is it's the beginning of freedom. It unlocks something in us that has been held hostage for a long time. It shows us we are safe, and I think it sends that energy out to everyone and everything around us.

When we are fully honest and accepting of everything that is within us, listening to ourselves with no judgment, that's when our walls drop and we feel hope, real hope. The love we give ourselves in that moment opens something up in us and in the universe that is palpable and healing.

Please know that what is in you is not scary. It is not bad. It is worth looking at, holding, and saying, *"It's okay. You can come out now. You're safe here."*

This is what allows the colors in our lives to deepen and our spirit to soar.

May you feel the freedom to feel all that is within you. You are worth being heard.

23

The Magic of Dropping Labels

Years ago I heard Eckhart Tolle point out how we label everything, and when we do that it takes away the magic of what we are looking at, what we are experiencing. He encouraged people to drop the labels and see how different that feels.

Whenever I do this, the difference in the way I feel and in the way I see things is amazing. For instance, if I look at a tree and decide to see it without the word "tree" attached to it, it becomes this amazing living miracle. I can feel it more. I feel love for it. I feel gratitude, connection, a calmness comes over me. I look at every part of it and feel in awe.

When my eyes go to the mountains I live by, I drop the word "mountain" and suddenly feel calm. They now look like a powerful, magical creature that is resting, living right by me. Feelings well up inside me as if the mountains have feelings. They feel loving to me. I feel the overwhelming sense we are all here together.

I'm sitting in Wesley Owens Coffee & Cafe in Monument, Colorado as I write this, looking out the window. I decide to look at a woman sitting at a nearby table talking with her partner. What if I didn't see her with the label of "woman" or "human" or "person"? The thing I notice when I do this is there is an immediate switch from my head to my feeling center. The core of me. Now when I look at her with no label, she feels miraculous. She feels like light. Bright iridescent light. Suddenly it feels like everyone here is family. We all feel like we are here together. I look around and feel love, a connection with everyone. A smile naturally forms on my face. I feel the sense that all the miraculous forces I see around me love me. It's quite profound. I feel relaxed.

I look over at my coat lying on the ottoman in front of me. I drop the "coat" label. Now it feels so beautiful. It feels like it has life to it. A personality. It lies so beautifully. It looks soft. The way the lining lies with its curves and folds seems so wonderful. So gentle. I feel so in love with this jacket right now. It feels like it loves taking care of me.

I know this may sound out there to some of you, but it really causes a big shift to happen inside us.

Whenever I take the time to do this, I see life differently. It feels like a friendly place that has only love for me. My body relaxes.

I feel tender toward everything I look at in this way. I feel tender toward myself. I feel the sense that everything is okay. It's all good. I feel so lucky to live in such an enchanted place.

It's a wonderful practice to do this to ourselves, too. I look at my fingers moving around on these keys and drop the label "fingers". They are amazing. Truly amazing. They dance like some beautiful creature I just discovered in a colorful land. I'm amazed by them, and it feels really good just to notice them, to put my attention on them.

It's a meditative practice that keeps you present and opens your eyes to things you don't normally see.

If we pay attention to our feet as we walk and drop the word "feet", they take on a whole new feeling. They now feel magical to me. Amazing. They feel creature-like, in a sense. I feel as if I have super powers.

Oh, I hope you try this today. It will change your feeling state. It will take you to a wonderful place inside yourself. You will feel different about yourself and the world around you. Welcome to your magical body and world you live in.

24

Rest

To rest is to become present in a different way than through action, and especially to give up on the will as the prime motivator of endeavor, with its endless outward need to reward itself through established goals. To rest is to give up on worrying and fretting and the sense that there is something wrong with the world unless we put it right.

-From "Consolations" by David Whyte

For some reason, rest has been a difficult thing for me to allow myself. I easily get caught up in fears of not accomplishing, not being productive, not using my time "wisely" to further my goals.

So when I rest I might think I'm wasting time, not moving ahead, or I'm lazy.

There is a frantic drive in many of us to keep going. Where are we going? We don't really know. Somewhere. Somewhere ahead of where we are now.

Resting does not have the feeling of moving forward. On the contrary, it has the movement of being right here, right now, in the present moment. It is a gift. It keeps us present, which for some of us is a scary thought because, in being, we feel. Things come up when we rest we don't have distractions to go to.

Whenever I get to the place where I give myself permission to rest, I never regret it. I usually feel a shift in my mind and my heart later, when I have moved on from resting. I feel more peaceful, calm, more connected to myself.

While I'm resting, it can feel like nothing is happening. The truth is a lot is happening within our bodies we can't see and sometimes aren't in touch with. In fact, often when I am feeling stuck, confused or stressed about a decision the best thing for me is to walk away from doing and lie down. Many times I receive the solution while lying there. Resting is like sacred space that ushers us into higher knowledge that is always inside of us and ready for us to access.

Our bodies know what we need.

I've had days where I've experimented with not having a to-do list, but just gone with what my body wanted, and I was amazed at how much I got done.

There are times I've rested for days and had this burst of productivity after that.

When my body is craving rest, I have the sense something is coming around the corner that I am being prepared for. It seems to be part of the rhythm of life. If we flow with what our body is asking for, we go with the current of the water rather than against it, and life takes on a feeling of ease and harmony. This is the way we were meant to walk this journey.

Life is about ebbs and flows. We go through different cycles, different seasons. The more we accept this and go with what our bodies are craving, the more we start to feel a settling in.

Resisting rest when our body is calling out for it keeps us in a state of unease. It becomes difficult to hear guidance and live our lives in harmony with who we are.

We were designed for a more peaceful existence.

As Doe Zantamata said, *"Taking time to do nothing often brings everything into perspective."*

Allowing yourself to have times of rest and letting those times be as long or as short as they need to be is a beautiful way of taking care of yourself, a way of living in partnership with your soul.

The next time you feel the need or desire to rest, I hope you accept the invitation. You will always be glad you did. Your body will thank you for it, and your soul will guide you through it.

25

Protecting Yourself

There is a book called *The Highly Sensitive Person: How to Thrive When the World Overwhelms You* by Elaine Aron. In it, you'll find a test to see if you are highly sensitive. There are twenty-two questions. If you answer "true" to more than twelve you are highly sensitive. Nineteen of them were true for me.

Being a highly sensitive person, I pick up on what other people are feeling. This can happen with people who are right beside me or a friend halfway around the world. I pick up on other's fearful thoughts and sometimes think they are my own. I have learned to say to myself, *"If any of these emotions or thoughts I'm feeling are not from me, I want you to leave right now. Only my thoughts and feelings are allowed in my body."* Many times after I say this I feel a sense of relief.

Through the years, I have researched different ways to protect myself from other people's negative energy because taking on that energy can suck my own. I've said different prayers that feel powerful to me. I have visualized various colored bubbles around me. Roses have the highest frequency of any plant on earth, I've been told, so I use them in visualizations as a form of protection.

When I was at a conference, a lady leading a seminar wanted to show the power of protecting yourself. She asked for a volunteer. She had the woman stand in the middle of a large circle of attendees. The moderator asked everyone in the circle to think loving thoughts, then she muscle strength tested the volunteer, and the volunteer's arm stayed strong.

Muscle strength testing is also called *applied kinesiology*—a technique used for many things, including discovering what things affect you, what things cause your body to be strong or go weak. For instance, some naturopathic doctors will have a patient hold a bottle of pills by their stomach and gently press their straightened arm down while the patient resists. If the arm stays strong, it is a message the body would do well with those pills. If the arm goes weak, the pills are not what the body wants. Our bodies are amazing, intelligent guides.

The moderator then told us to think negative, angry thoughts. When we did, she tested the woman, and the woman's arm went weak. The volunteer was clearly affected by other's negative thoughts and feelings, as we all are.

What happened after that was fascinating. She told the volunteer to close her eyes and see herself standing on a cement platform surrounded by a fountain with water shooting up around her. While she held that visual, we were supposed to think angry, hateful thoughts again. This time her body stayed strong. It was a powerful demonstration of how we can protect our bodies in a room filled with negative energy.

There are so many effective ways to be our own spiritual/energetic bodyguard, but I have been noticing something in myself that is feeling like the most powerful, natural, and gentle way of protecting myself.

The more I live my life loving myself, the more I notice other people don't affect me as much. The more I consciously connect with myself, stay inside my body, and speak kindly to myself, the more I notice this integrating with me and being less affected by the energy outside myself.

Sometimes it's a choice I make, and sometimes it just naturally happens.

I liken it to what makes a tree strong and solid, immovable—the root system under the tree. The more we build up our foundation, our core, our essence, the stronger and more solid we become. Loving ourselves can sound like a warm, fuzzy thing and not be associated with strength, power, and protection when, in fact, I believe it is the most powerful force we have.

There is a technique you can use to actually physically overpower someone by thinking loving thoughts. I have done this with big, strong men who could physically take me down in a heartbeat, and left them dumbfounded when they couldn't overpower me because I was picturing things like puppies and babies as I gently pushed their hands together while they tried with all their might to resist me.

I had an appointment with a woman this morning and started noticing my body tightening, my throat closing up, and me gradually leaving my body. The things she was saying and the way she was saying them were affecting me. When I noticed this, as she kept talking I spoke to myself internally and said, *"I'm here."* I felt my body relax instantly. I reassured myself that I don't have to do anything this lady is telling me to do. I am in charge. I was starting to think bleak thoughts when listening to her, so I gave myself a quick smile, letting myself know this is temporary and it's okay to feel whatever I'm feeling. I could feel myself coming back into my body and calming down.

I ended the meeting early. I actually started gathering my things and standing up as she continued to talk. I took care of myself. I checked in. I reconnected.

After I left, I took a moment to breathe. I could still feel her energy and said things to release it from my body. After that, I noticed I didn't feel anything negative toward her. Because I took care of myself, I was able to move on quickly and feel grateful for her taking the time to talk to me. I felt loving toward her as a human being on her own journey.

Since I've made connecting and loving myself a more consistent practice, I have noticed other times when I don't need to do anything. The more I walk through the day loving myself, the more I notice how much I naturally feel love inside me. When I feel filled with love, I see how easy and natural it is to treat others with kindness, to want to show love, and how natural it becomes to let them own their issues and not take them on myself.

When I get caught up in being irritated with other people, I leave my body. When I choose to stay in my body, I notice I am able to separate myself from others in a healthy way. I am able to see they have issues, too, and to let their issues be theirs. I am able to appreciate things about them that feel good and to listen to what I need and act on it.

Can you imagine having the full trust in yourself to take care of you? The more you make it a habit, loving yourself in a proactive way, the more evidence your brain will have that you can be trusted. The more your brain believes this through a new neural pathway you are developing, the more your nervous system will relax. When all that happens, there is a tremendous amount of peace that begins to reside in your body as your natural state. When this happens, you don't feel like you need protection. You are protected; you can feel it, living in such a safe environment that is your mind and body. You have the ability to create the safest place possible to live inside yourself.

The more you meet yourself with tenderness and care, the more you will be able to walk in this world with ease and freedom.

26

My Prayer Tonight

There are times when stressful thoughts and feelings come to me as I'm getting ready for bed. That is what I'm experiencing right now. My body feels tight and emotions are rising. I feel like I have a lot of thoughts in my head that are causing me to feel stress.

I just turned on the song *A Hundred Thousand Angels,* sung by Lucinda Drayton, and am playing it as I write. It calms me. I am realizing my thoughts and feelings need to be voiced.

I am often reminded that unseen beings are with me at all times, mainly because I feel them, I sense their presence wherever I am. I've been having conversations with them for years. It helps me to tell them everything. It feels like they want me to. When I sense them, I feel love and a desire to help me.

I don't know who they are, to be honest. They could be God, Jesus, angels, spirit guides, my mom, names I've never heard before. I don't need a label anymore. I know how they feel. They always, always, always feel loving. I feel complete freedom to be myself around them and to say anything. I feel no judgment from them, only unconditional acceptance. I weep around them, ask them questions, and often hear answers, or receive what I would describe as *intuitive knowing*. There have been times I yelled at them and there have been times I sang to them, as well as times I cried because I felt so loved and supported. I feel embraced, known, connected, and seen when I am in their presence.

I usually refer to them as angels because I have always loved the idea of angels.

When stressful thoughts come to me at night, I am very tired and just don't feel like helping myself through intellectual means, like looking at my thoughts to see what's causing me stress. I go with what feels soothing and caretaking in the moment. I go with what I crave and oftentimes that is connection.

So tonight as I tuck myself in, I feel like connecting with my unseen helpers. I feel like laying everything out and asking for help—

Angels, this is what I'm feeling right now. I'm feeling things around _____. I'm scared of _____. I'm also scared that _____. I feel hurt that _____. I feel sad about _____.

I ask for your help right now with all these things. I want to recognize truth. I want to be clear about the areas that feel jumbled and confusing. I want to find and experience peace with all of it. I want to see clearly instead of feeling lost.

I want to let go of thoughts and ingrained beliefs that are keeping me frozen, holding me back from being myself and doing what I came here to do.

I ask for your help now in reminding me of who I am and why I am here. I want to see easily what I need to see at this moment.

Please do what is in your power to help me with all these things.

Thank you for being here. Thank you for helping. Thank you for loving me and knowing me in ways I cannot see.

I wanted to share this prayer with you in the hope that it would help you during those times you feel lost and not sure what to say. I also wanted to remind you that you are not alone on this journey. You have a host of unseen helpers who love you more than you could imagine.

May you feel comforted and loved today. May you come to the realization your divine helpers are ready and willing to help with whatever you need and long for. May you be able to feel the peace that resides within you and is connected to others around you. You were made for peace and connection. May you recognize how valued you are today.

27

The Sheep and the Farmer

Sometimes a sheep accidentally takes a plunge into the water. Its wool soaks up the water and gets so heavy it's almost impossible for a person to drag the sheep out. *"It happens quite often,"* a farmer told a colleague of mine. She asked him what he did in that situation, knowing he wouldn't just let the sheep drown.

His answer was simple and profound, *"People always want to rush things. They want to solve all problems, and they need to solve them NOW. What I do is the opposite. I do practically nothing. I get into the water and let the animal lean on me. I can sense when it gets calmer. When that happens, the sheep takes a leap and scrambles ashore all by itself. I only give it the tiniest push."*

Tears came to my eyes hearing this because it was a picture of the way I have been living my life lately.

I reached a point where I felt physically and emotionally weighed down by painful experiences, by thoughts that have caused me to feel fear and anxiety for years, by the stresses of the society I live in, and by years of busy-ness.

I have needed to step off this train. During this time, I have been treating myself like the farmer gently helps his soaked sheep. I have been allowing myself to just be, to stay in the water and lean on myself. I have become someone I can lean on. I have become a safe presence for me to admit all my thoughts and feelings.

I am not ready to come out of the water yet. I can feel that I need to stay here a little longer. For years I have pushed myself to do things without listening and honoring my feelings. I have not always taken care of myself. I have not always been a safe place where I could lean.

I also intuitively know a time will come for me to walk out of the water. I will instinctively know when. I will want to come out. At that time, when I am calm enough inside myself, I will feel the tiniest nudge and will leave the water and enter life again. It will be different this time.

Having given myself this space to be and to nurture myself, I will be able to reenter the world with strength, stillness, and profound kindness wherever I go and however I decide to leave my imprint in this world.

The day will come when I will be ready to take the leap, and it will feel amazing.

Give yourself what you need, lovely. If you are feeling weighed down, allow yourself time to lean until you feel that inner calmness. You are worth the time, worth the care. Stay in the water for as long as you need to. Know that the time will come when you will be ready to leap. Your tenderness is magnificent. Take care of that precious heart of yours.

28

What to Do with the Stories

Our minds spin stories a lot, and most of the time they are stories that cause us to feel painful and stressful emotions. We have stories around whether we will be successful or end up broke and alone. We spin stories about the financial future of our countries.

The other day I heard a man going on and on about how hard the future is going to be for the next generation. He spun a lot of stories as to why it's going to be really hard for them to find jobs. Is it? Do we know this for sure?

We tell others and ourselves stories about health and weight loss.

We spin stories about our kids: *What if they are doing this? What if this happens to them?* And on and on.

What about our aging parents?

What about a sibling who seems to be making really bad decisions?

What should we do? How do we fix these things? Ahhhhh!!!

I do it, too. We all do. I was just on a walk behind my house observing my thoughts going wild over a couple of topics I tend to replay often. The more time I spend going over all the analysis like I do with these stories, the tighter my body feels.

When we keep telling others and ourselves these stories, we leave our bodies. After all, who would want to stay in a body filled with stressful thoughts?

I decided to lie down on the grassy hill during my walk, look at the clouds, and ask myself one question: What am I feeling?

When we stop the stories and focus on the feelings, amazing things happen.

When I do this, I notice I am back in my body. I stick with only feelings, not thoughts. I keep asking: *What am I feeling?* Fear. Anxiety… *What else?* Frustration… *What else?*

The more I state the feelings out loud, the more I notice my body and my mind calming down.

When we focus on the story, our feelings stay bottled up inside. When we say what we are feeling they are allowed to come out, and trust is built because we are listening, acknowledging, and being with our sweet, scared selves.

Another thing I've noticed about this is when we keep telling the story we remain the powerless victim, which never feels good. When we acknowledge the emotions we are no longer the victim, we are not powerless, we are not dependent on circumstances changing so we can feel better. We are now in the driver's seat and can affect change just by being really honest with ourselves and allowing the feelings to come up and be acknowledged.

So the next time you notice yourself going over and over some topic in your mind, be aware this is just a story. In that moment, I hope you allow yourself to go to your feelings. Let them be heard and love them. Be with them. They are just feelings.

You are worth taking the time to be heard. You are worthy of peace, worthy of calm.

Be the safe space for yourself that you so deserve.

29

Being Your Own Hero

Lying on a hammock in my backyard, looking up at the sky, I was just thinking about how I recently told a friend of mine he was my hero because he had figured out how to support himself while traveling the world. Then I thought about how often I lift others up higher than myself. I look around at what other adults are doing with their lives and am so impressed with how they seem to have figured this life out.

This thinking gets me into trouble, because when I lift others up I tend to idealize them and see them as knowing more than I do, lessening who I am and how I have impacted this world just by being here. I end up belittling the way I have lived my life when, in fact, the things I have brought to this world, to my kids, to friends and family, are so valuable. I buy into the illusion that what someone does or has created defines them and gives them value.

Then a thought came to me: *I am my own hero right now.* I smiled at this idea and started listing for myself all the ways I see myself as a hero:

I've been through painful things and still remain tender.

I have faithfully taken care of my kids during times when I wanted to run away and do my own thing.

I am brave enough to be honest about my true thoughts and feelings.

I am taking the time to be with myself and to love myself more than ever before.

I am a kind person.

I am doing things outside of my comfort zone.

I have been really honest with people when it wasn't easy.

I have become much more honest with myself than I used to be.

I am learning to trust myself.

It did something wonderful, healing to my soul when I started listing off these things. It wasn't from ego, making myself higher than someone else. It was acknowledging the parts of me I'm really proud of and impressed by.

I'm not sure why we shy away from that. I think we've adopted this idea that if we focus on ourselves, lift ourselves up, we become self-focused when, in fact, the opposite is true. When we take the time to do this, our nervous system calms. We feel more relaxed and filled with love, which ends up making us a more loving and compassionate person to others.

If you find yourself doing the same thing I've done for years, putting other people above you, I hope you can take a moment to write down or think about all the ways you are your own hero.

There are things about you, often little things you do, ways that you are, that are heroic. Thank you for the beautiful things you bring to this world.

Thank you for taking the time to love on yourself. You doing this changes your energy and, in turn, affects the people and world around you, and we thank you for that.

The Safest Place Possible

30

What Do You REALLY Want?

What is it you really want to do with your life? I mean REALLY want to do?

What kind of life are you aching to live?

One way of creating the safest space for you to live in is to allow yourself to be really honest about what it is you really want.

I've spent a lot of years doing things that made me money, things that I could do, that I have the capability of doing. Some jobs were tolerable, some were somewhat enjoyable, and some I really liked but wouldn't want to do for the rest of my life.

I've pursued things I knew I would succeed at, other things I thought I'd make good money doing.

There are many things I enjoy. I love traveling. I like writing. I love spending time with friends. I love staying in nice hotels, watching TV shows like *House Hunters International* and *The Voice*. I love eating popcorn while watching a good movie. I love almost any kind of boating. I like decorating. I love swimming, biking, and dancing. I love learning about life and about how to experience more peace. I love going on retreats. Did I mention I really love popcorn?

Career-wise I've done a variety of work. I've been an event coordinator, a janitor, a bus person, and a hostess at Chi-Chi's Tex-Mex Restaurant and Bar. I've flipped homes, worked in different retail shops, was a camp counselor, and had a short stint as a real estate agent. I worked in advertising, event planning, was an assistant director for a musical, started my own coupon book business, answered phones as a receptionist, and worked various jobs at a conference center. I took a life-changing course to become a life coach and loved it! That's been my plan the past couple of years, to have life coaching be my career. I know I'm good at it and enjoy it. I get excited about ideas like facilitating retreats, and I'll start pursuing one part of it but then lose interest. I've wondered why.

There is one desire, however, one dream I've had for a very long time. I have dabbled in, played with, pursued it here and there, but never really admitted to myself that this, above all else, is what my heart is affected by most. The thought of doing this for the rest of my life fills me and relaxes me like nothing else does. It brings tears to my eyes.

I haven't been totally honest with myself about this until recently. I think because it has always felt so lofty to me, so unattainable. It also scares me because it is so close to my heart, but now it feels like a need. An urgency, in a way. I am feeling I must do this. I cannot keep going on with life not doing this. I feel it rising in me more than ever. It feels like a calling within me.

Recently I took on a job to make money and to build a career through. The idea I had was to do life coaching on the side but, just in case that doesn't pan out for me, this career would be my alternative, guaranteed income. That was a good plan in theory, but when I am at this job I feel flat inside. The energy inside me feels stagnant. Dormant. Fear fills me proclaiming, *"This is what I'm doing now? This is what my life looks like now and for a very long time?"* I sink into despair and am unable to see clearly. I have four years to make a go of it until my marital support comes to an end, so I got a backup job just in case I don't succeed. For me, taking this job at the beginning helped me feel relief. I felt like I had a safety net. But the longer I'm there, the more I feel unhappy and a little more fearful.

The wonderful thing about me being so unhappy is it was pushing me to ask the question, "Debbie, what is it you really want to do? If you really could do something that you would really enjoy, that would feel fulfilling, life-giving to you, what would that look like?" If I was going to put my time and energy into a job that depleted me, why not put that time and energy into a life I would actually enjoy? Even if I failed, at least I would always know I gave it a chance. When I was pushed to be really honest, my buried dream came rising up.

I want to sing.

I want to create beautiful, healing, calming, loving, original music. I want to sing songs that help people feel loved, uplifted, and calm. I want to create a space with music that helps bring love and healing to people; a space where they will be able to hear their hearts, to reconnect with their beautiful selves.

So I am now paying attention to this cry of my soul, to this leading of my heart.

This is something I was born to do. It is one reason I came here. I was given a gift and a strong desire, and because I have those in me I know it is possible.

So, beautiful one, what is your buried dream? What is your heart longing to do?

I am now going to fire away with some great life coaching questions for you to ponder—

Who are you jealous of and why?

What things did you play as a child and adolescent? (My sister and I used to stand in my dad's home office with earmuffs on, holding a round brush, telling "Jack" to turn up the bass as we simulated recording an album in a studio.)

Our lives are filled with clues as to why we are here.

What do you find yourself doing where you lose track of time?

What stories do you like to hear about how certain people got to where they are?

Who seems like they have such a great life? What appears great about their life to you?

If you could magically create a life with your rules, what would it look like?

What books, articles, and TV shows do you gravitate to?

What are you scared to say out loud that you really would like to do with your life?

What imprint do you want to leave on this earth?

It's time. It's time to be really honest. It's time to honor yourself, your desires, your dreams.

You don't have to figure out how yet. All you need to do now is say out loud, or write down, what it is you really want to do.

Give yourself that freedom, that safe place. Embrace yourself through this. It takes courage.

You deserve to live a life that is in harmony with how you are made, with what you need, with what works for you.

You will feel different inside when you voice what you really want. You may feel fear, excitement, or both. Tears might come. The more you embrace this, own it, claim it, the more you will feel a strength within you that is your true self, your true essence.

You are here for a reason. You have something very special about you. I wish I could hear about it right now. I wish we could all sit in a circle and hear each other's precious dreams.

Know that you are not alone. I and many others are smiling right now, thinking about you doing what you long to do. I'm a big fan and can't wait to see you shine.

31

What If

What if what you think is wrong with you is actually what makes you really special and needed in this world?

What if you knew you were never alone, that you have unseen helpers who love you beyond belief?

What if you knew the world was for you?

What if everything was stacked in your favor?

What if seeing yourself as beautiful was as natural as breathing and you couldn't imagine seeing yourself any other way?

What if you fully trusted your own intuition?

What if you could be okay with every feeling that comes your way?

What if your body was the safest place for your sensitive heart to live?

What if you loved everything about who you are?

What if being alone felt like curling up with a warm blanket and smiling from the inside out?

What if fear was something you remember feeling in the past but can't imagine feeling again?

What if you already have all the answers you need inside you?

What if you didn't need to accomplish anything to feel valuable?

What if the idea of speaking to yourself in an unkind way was a distant memory and you could never imagine speaking to yourself in that way again?

What if you knew you were always in the right place at the right time?

What if you knew that being your honest self helps everyone around you, even if they are not aware?

What if you don't have to do things perfectly for things to work out?

It is possible to live life knowing and feeling these thoughts.

It is possible to have these so ingrained in you that you can't imagine believing anything different.

Keep loving yourself.

Keep treating yourself with kindness and gentleness, and your life will change forever.

Allow yourself to be led by your own inner guidance. It knows what you need.

The source of that voice is for you and loves you unconditionally.

What if you knew this to be true and felt the peace of this with every breath?

The Safest Place Possible

32

I Adore You

Dear Reader,

You are my hero right now.

You are my hero because you take the time to love yourself, and by doing that you have helped heal the world around you.

You are my hero because you are brave enough to feel your feelings and courageous enough to be really honest.

You are my hero because you are wise enough to see the value of creating a safe space for your heart.

May you feel proud of yourself in this moment.

May you know that you are loved.

May you experience the depth of joy and peace that exists within you and all around you.

May every breath you take breathe love into every part of you.

May you continue to feel what you were made for.

May you live a life that reflects the beauty and authenticity of your heart.

Take care of your heart, my friend. When your heart happy, more happy come to you.

May you have the bravery, the courage, to let yourself experience more happiness.

I love you. I adore you. I applaud you, and I am with you.

Thank you. Thank you for caring about your heart.

Thank you for being brave.

I see you and honor you.

With so much love and respect,

Debbie